THE
INTERIOR
WAY

BY
JEANNE GUYON

THE
INTERIOR
WAY

Published by:

The SeedSowers
P.O. Box 3317
Jacksonville, FL 32206
1-800-228-2665
www.seedsowers.com

Library of Congress Cataloging - in - Publication Data
Copyright MMII
by
Edwards, Gene
The Interior Way
ISBN 0-940232-86-3
1. Spiritual

Times New Roman 13pt.

Acknowledgment

Years ago the publishers wanted to place in print the book *Union with God*, by Jeanne Guyon, but the vocabulary of the English translation was so extremely obscure that the book defied modernization or even interpretation. At that time we called on Helen Edwards to use her formidable skills to bring that book out of abject obscurity into the light of modern English. The result was the recovery of a great book, and it was a tour de force on the part of Helen.

Bringing *The Interior Way* into a manageable modernization was a challenge even greater than the one found in *Union with God*. Once more we turned to Helen. She spent hundreds of hours working on this book.

Helen's counterpart in this undertaking was Phil Warmanen, whom we have often turned to for help in editing our books. He shares in the acknowledgment for the long hours and tenacious labor he rendered in editing *The Interior Way*.

Without Helen and Phil, this book might have lain dormant forever. We acknowledge a great debt to them in issuing *The Interior Way*.

We also offer our deep appreciation to Mary Rodriguez for typing the edited manuscript and to Nicole DeGier for her skills and labor in typesetting.

The Publishers

Books by Jeanne Guyon

Experiencing the Depths of Jesus Christ
Final Steps in Christian Maturity
Intimacy with Christ
Spiritual Torrents
Union with God
Autobiography of Jeanne Guyon

Commentaries by Jeanne Guyon

Genesis
Exodus
Leviticus - Numbers - Deuteronomy
Judges
Job
Song of Songs
Jeremiah
James - First John - Revelation

also

The Life of Jeanne Guyon *(T.C. Upham)*

Table of Contents

Note from the Editors

This book is a compilation of writings selected by Jeanne Guyon in the seventeenth century, and also includes excerpts from books of her own authorship. This compilation was originally known as Guyon's *Justifications*. She was called on by the Catholic Church to justify her spiritual teachings. She felt she had thoroughly justified her teachings by referring to Scripture and to the writings of Catholic authors of her day and earlier in history. Nevertheless, she was imprisoned in the Bastille, in a time when the Catholic Church had the power to imprison or execute anyone whose teachings did not conform to Catholic doctrine.

The original French this book was cast in was medieval French. In order for the modern reader to grasp the context, it was necessary to take some editing liberties. Hopefully, it will inspire you to a deeper walk with your Lord.

Please do not struggle to place yourself in one of the stages of spiritual growth that these writers try to delineate. Remember, these are their testimonies, and it is not necessary for you to have the same experiences they had. We are recording their experiences as an important part of history, and we believe these testimonies will be useful to most readers in their walk with the Lord.

Within the covers of this book are to be found many spiritual riches—but they may have to be sought diligently and carefully to be obtained.

Some readers may not feel it is necessary to read the entire book. Others, however, are especially interested in everything that Guyon wrote.

We believe we have produced for you a readable book that is faithful to the intended messages of the authors. You will find some flavor still intact from the medieval language of the Catholic Church of that age.

When editing the writings of Jeanne Guyon, there is always the desire to use the pronoun *she* to refer to an unnamed believer. However, we have chosen to use the pronoun *he*, in keeping with common practice and with the style of our own publications. We have, in some of our earlier books, apologized for this difficulty where some readers might like to see the pronoun *she*. There are, however, some places where the authors have intermingled references to the believer with references to the Bride, so these we usually refer to as *she*. And we even used *he or she* a few times.

These ancient writers used *the soul* to refer to an unnamed individual. We have changed *the soul* to *the believer* or *a Christian*, etc. They used *the creature* to refer to a human being or other created things. We have changed this according to the way it was used.

The Story Behind This Book

The year was 1694, and France was turned on its ear by two archbishops. They were dueling verbally over a woman!

To be specific, both men were publishing pamphlets about the writings of Jeanne Guyon. One of these men, Fenelon, was a friend of Jeanne Guyon. The other one, Bossuet, was attacking her. (Both men were archbishops!) They were not only the two best-know clergymen of France in that day, but they are the two best-known archbishops in all of French history.

Louise XIV wanted Guyon silenced. So did his wife Mme. de Maintenon. Bossuet was the one who rose to do the king's bidding. Fenelon, the other most famous (and certainly the most revered) clergyman, rose to defend Jeanne Guyon. Bossuet accused Guyon of *novel teachings*. This is a serious charge because it is just one step lower than a charge of heresy. (He later changed his accusation to include heresy.) Guyon was removed to a town called Meaux, which was in Bossuet's parish. She was held there, under house arrest, until such time as a theological investigation could be made of her writings and of her life.

Two of her books would be examined by this investigation: *Experiencing the Depths of Jesus Christ** and *The Song of Songs*.

Archbishop Jacques Bossuet was expected to become the archbishop of the city of Paris. The present archbishop was frail and in poor health. Everyone knew Bossuet would be Paris's next archbishop. It was virtually certain that he would one day wear the hat of a cardinal. Three priests including Bossuet were to examine Guyon in what was essentially an ecclesiastical trial. Bossuet was certain that he could dispatch this woman without any great problem. Like everyone else, he underestimated this French lady. (During the questioning she trounced all three of her examiners. Bossuet was furious.)

Let us look at this story in a little bit more detail.

Guyon was told to go to the city of Meaux and await her examination. She was there a long time—long enough to win the admiration of the nuns in the convent where she was staying. During this time Guyon was given a list of topics upon which she was to be questioned. She, in turn, used this time not only to review the questions but to write out in full her view on each of these topics. She did this in order to express to the three priests that her teachings were consistent with those who, in the past, were considered great people of Christ. Guyon researched the writings of all of these highly respected people who had lived before her. She quoted their writings extensively and compared their words with her own. She called this work her *Justifications*. That is, she was saying in this manuscript that she was justified in her teaching and that her writings agreed perfectly with the most revered Catholics of the past. Bossuet, though he had a titanic mind, knew virtually nothing of the writings of these devotees of Christ. He was a logical, intellectual theologian; and that was all that he was. In fact Bossuet was shocked to hear that a deeper experience with Christ, outside of church ritual, was possible.

---

* The original title of this book was *A Short and Simple Way to Pray*. Today this classic of all classics is known as *Experiencing the Depths of Jesus Christ* (Published by SeedSowers Publishing House).

Guyon told Bossuet that the writings of these great figures clearly indicated that they were not special people nor did they have special revelation, but rather testified that a knowledge of an indwelling Lord was available for all who believed in Christ. Bossuet was dumbfounded.

Nonetheless, Bossuet held to his task. He was to learn nothing from Guyon nor from the great figures of church history who had come before. His task was to silence Jeanne Guyon and to show her books as being contrary to the church.

The names of the three priests who examined Guyon were: Tronson, de Noaoailles, and Bossuet. Because Tronson was frail in health, the examination would be held in his country estate, St. Sulpice, rather than in Meaux. His estate was near a town called Issy, and Issy was near Paris. (History was later to give the name of this inquisition the title *The Issy Conference*.)

This examination took a total of nine months. It began in July of 1694 and did not end until March of 1695. It appeared that life imprisonment for Guyon was a certainty. Bossuet was after a sensational and triumphant condemnation of Guyon, with a view to adding one more victory to his already illustrious career. There was reason behind this that had nothing to do with things spiritual. The archbishop of Paris was, as stated, old and frail. Bossuet was certain he would be the next archbishop of Paris and therefore the closest clergyman in France to the throne of Louis XIV.

Fortunately, there were many other forces at work during this period in France, forces which denied Bossuet his dream.

At the end of the Issy Conference, Guyon played the ultimate card. She submitted herself and her writings to the Archbishop of Paris! Although he was an elderly man, he was a wise man. His name was Archbishop Harlay. When Harlay officially censored Guyon, she quickly submitted to him and to the church. For all legal purposes the battle was over, and the whole matter should have ended there.

Bossuet was a vengeful man, capable of virtually any move that would favor his desires. Even though the Issy examination was over, Bossuet would not allow Guyon to leave Meaux. For the rest of the year 1695, he badgered her, tormented her, accused her, and condemned her. He was still wanting her books and her teachings condemned, even if he had to go all the way to Rome and to the pope. There was a short moment when he relented; he set Jeanne Guyon free. There is no known reason for this, except for what happened next. Bossuet accused Guyon of *escaping* from Meaux. She was now a fugitive. Near the end of 1695, Jeanne Guyon was arrested and sent to the fortress-prison in the city of Vincennes, a city located on the outskirts of Paris. She was later transferred to the infamous Bastille.

Today few people remember Bossuet, fewer still remember Mme. de Maintenon. But what of Fenelon and Guyon? Guyon is the second most-read author of the 1600's. Only William Shakespeare, who also lived during the sixteen hundreds, is read more than Jeanne Guyon. Fenelon, too, is remembered for his ever-popular work now entitled *The Seeking Heart**. The influence of these two people increases with every passing generation.

---

*Published by SeedSowers Publishing House

What good came out of the Conference of Issy? The answer is simple. The writings of Jeanne Guyon which she called her *Justifications*. That is what came forth from this ordeal.

We have therefore given the background to this book. This book is no longer called *Justifications* but is now entitled *The Interior Way*. It is the fond hope of the publisher that you will find insight in this mammoth work that will give light and phrases which were popular as far back as A.D. 1200.

Jeanne Guyon, writing in the 1600's, used language that was only a little less obscure than did those who came before her.

You may wish to read *The Interior Way* all the way through. On the other hand, we would like to suggest that you consider using *The Interior Way* as a devotional book, reading only a few pages each day. Either way, you will have the privilege of reading the writings of people who lived in an era stretching from A.D. 1200 to A.D. 1600 . . . who are among the most devout believers of that era.

The Publishers

Comments by Jeanne Guyon

Jeanne Guyon was handed a list of subjects and told to express her opinion about them. (She added a number of her own!) She wrote the following words concerning her own writings, testimony, justifications: I say things as they come to me, not knowing whether I put it right or not. When I write them, they seem to me as clear as daylight. Later I see them as things that I have never known, and I cannot believe that I have written them. I pray God, if such is His wish, to make people understand what I cannot express better. Although one writes about the higher stages of the internal life, it does not mean one believes that he or she has reached these stages.

The subject of this book is the holy Love which must not be judged through words and through the tongue. It can be judged only through its truths. If someone wants to reach the state I have described he must love. Otherwise, the one who does not love will approach vainly to understand or to read this song of love, because an icy heart cannot understand the words that are afire. In the same way as one who does not know Greek will not understand those who speak it, the language of love will sound barbaric to the one who does not love.

I submitted purely and simply my writings. Although I do not care what will become of them, I owe truth to make known the fact that they agree with the doctors sanctioned by the Church. The work I am doing in this matter is only to make the truth better known, and to make it better known without pretending to bother regarding the fate of my writings, declaring that I am not interested in them any more and that I will never ask what has happened to them. This being so, I am going to relate the propositions in my printed books with those of the serious authors who wrote similar truths. I do not do it to back up my opinions but to make truths clearer. I ask earnestly that all my writings should be examined. The *Song of Songs* was a continuation of previous writings, and one is supposed to have read the preceding writings. It is in all these writings that my feelings are explained more in detail, in one place or another, so that one can judge correctly my thoughts and my faith.

So it was that Guyon began her defense.

Author's Introduction

The essence of the Christian life is to love God with all our hearts, praying continuously, and to bear our cross every day. The Gospels present divine love as the fulfillment of the Law. The way to reach that stage of love is by continuous prayer and abandoning self.

Pure Love

God loves Himself supremely and uniquely because He is supremely and uniquely loveworthy. God's perfection is the rule of His love. Therefore, the most perfect rule of man's finite will is, without doubt, the rule of God's infinite will. One may dispute, one may be very subtle about it, one may even propose as many arguments as possible on a theme different from love, but nobody will ever dare to deny that the supreme rule of love must be to love God for Himself and everything for His sake.

The hope of seeing God is a legitimate reason for love, a source of infinite comfort, and a powerful bulwark against all the temptations and miseries of our temporal existence. But this is not pure love. The Scriptures make a distinction between the two virtues, hope and love. We must not confuse them, nor reject one in preference for the other. As man is not the true light which illuminates his spirit, in the same way he is not the cause of the perfect love which moves his will. A power superior to man must act ceaselessly in him in order to raise him above himself and cause him to love according to the eternal law of love.

Prayer

First of all, the believer is moved by God's grace, and his will is pushed to try to abandon self and turn to God. After being accustomed for a long time to frequent lapses, the believer little by little becomes accustomed to living more simply, more intimately, and more evenly. The believer acts, but God alone is the principle of his action. He Himself moves the believer, propels him forward, animates him, and trains him; and the believer responds and is pushed forward. It is not an idleness of the believer, neither is it necessarily a cooperation, but rather a free agreement to the will of God. The more the believer agrees with God, the more vigorously the will of God responds. And both come together as bodies which fall toward a center.

Sacrifice

As man completes this union with God through prayer, he runs away from the world and from himself by renouncement—which is the second way to experience union with God.

This renouncement or sacrifice is *not* a form of austerity which surpasses human strength, destroys health, and makes one lead an extraordinary life. Jesus Christ did not practice that kind of austerity. His life outwardly was like everyone else's, but inwardly He was all divine. The renouncement which He inspires makes us not only avoid false pleasures, fight our coarse passions, and be content simply with what we are and have, but it also causes us to avoid all frivolous entertainment, all activities of the mind, and all the flights of imagination which only seem to dissipate our attention and to maintain in us the love of the world. This renouncement causes us to reject the slightest involvements with anything outside of God, the smallest pleasure against His commands, and the slightest return to vain complacencies towards oneself. It makes us love silence, inner solitude amongst the noise of the crowd, poverty of spirit, and perfect abnegation amidst wealth. This is not all. This abnegation tends to degrade the self, an idol which is so dear to man, and leads us to accept with joy what crucifies us. Then we can bear both other people's imperfections with patience and sweetness, as well as our own faults with peace and humility. This is a death which involves the senses, the brain, the heart, the entire man, and which leaves no place for the wild love of the world or of oneself.

The Inner Life

All mysteries of inner life can be found in this continuous prayer and in this yieldedness to God. Continuous prayer is like a sweet emotion and is full of charms. It tends to make the believer respond and try to get detached from things. This longing is the basis of inner life, without which all manner of spirituality is suspect. Then God starts to work on the believer in a different way. The believer becomes completely passive; he cooperates with God by not resisting. God alone can annihilate the self. The believer does not have to fight external things anymore. God attacks him from inside so he can die to the self. He shows the believer the inner recesses of his heart and his self-esteem. He unveils all the secrets. The believer then sees himself and abhors what he sees. Everything in him rises against the self. He no longer finds any comfort in his former piety nor in his own justice. God has shown him how impure he is. He swoons. All he has left is the firm will to suffer a thousand deaths rather than displease God. Sometimes he does not have the comfort of feeling even that much will in action. God's work in him continues to become more deep-seated, more intimate, and more central. The believer feels as if he is disappearing more and more, but he is still real.

The Aims of God

Our self-esteem, having lost its taste for impure pleasures and material objects as well as coarse passions, would create for itself a new empire for its own virtues, would be happy in its own excellence, and would corrupt the work of God by subtle self-indulgence. Perhaps one would not commit overt, coarse sins, but the subtler sins of pride and empty complacency. That is why the most advanced states of spiritual life are filled with temptations, deprivations, uncertainties, desolations, inner sufferings, and an unfulfilled heart, until the reign of self-love is annihilated and the rule of God inside is established.

The Next Stage of a Spiritual Life

Then the many, tumultuous, vague thoughts and the unruled passions, which put natural man into an everlasting frenzy, come to an end. The spirit is delivered from all needless activities, the will is free from all disquieting perturbations, and the person is reduced to a peace, to an emptiness, and to a divine solitude in which the senses and the imagination are quiet and able to listen to God's voice. God speaks to the heart, not through visions, nor revelations, nor sublime lights, but through much more perfect language, which is less subject to illusions.

God is everything and man is nothing, and he is compelled to deep homage to the all-powerful God. Then man does not live his own life anymore, but Jesus Christ lives in him. He is reborn and becomes as a child. The light of Christ becomes his only light and the love of the Holy Spirit his only love. His life is hidden in God with Jesus Christ, and this new life replaces the former life of Adam. This is the regeneration mentioned in the Gospel. These are the three states of the spiritual life which some mystics call purgative, illuminative, and unitive, and which I call active, passive, and divine. To express it in another way: They are renouncing false vices, destroying self-love, and reestablishing divine order by pure love.

Justification of two of my books:

A Short and Simple Way to Pray
and
The Song of Songs*

I submitted purely and simply my writings. Although I do not care what will become of them, I owe truth to make known the fact that they agree with the doctors sanctioned by the Church. The work I am doing in this matter is only to make the truth better known, and to make it better known without pretending to bother regarding the fate of my writings, declaring that I am not interested in them any more and that I will never ask what has happened to them. This being so, I am going to relate the propositions in my printed books with those of serious authors who have written the same things. I do not do it simply to support my opinions but to make truths clearer. I ask earnestly that all my writings should be examined. The *Song of Songs* was a continuation of previous writings, and one is supposed to have read the preceding writings. It is in all these writings that my feelings are explained more in detail in one place or another, so that one can judge correctly my thoughts and my faith.

---

* The book formerly entitled *A Short and Simple Way* to Pray is now called *Experiencing the Depths of Jesus Christ. The Song of Songs* is now entitled *The Song of the Bride*. Both are published by SeedSowers Publishing House.

1

ABANDONMENT

I submit the following topics I have written on in
A Short and Simple Way to Pray
and other writings

Believers who abandon themselves to God will give to Him their hearts and their freedom, so He can do what He will.

Be patient in prayer. If you should never do anything else in your life but wait for the return of the Beloved, patiently and with a humble spirit, abandoned, resigned and happy, then Oh! what wonderful prayer it would be. That is where giving everything up to God and consecrating everything to Him begins. I implore you, whoever you are, you who have decided to give yourself to God, do not take yourself back once you have given yourself to Him. Abandonment is the key of the whole inner life. Therefore, you must be firm in your abandon without listening to reason nor thought. If you would truly give yourself to God, you must trust in God.

Abandonment is a divesting of all care for ourselves, indeed it is giving up ourselves to be led by God. All Christians are asked to do this. There must be renouncement for the inner as well as the outer life, giving oneself totally into the hands of God, forgetting all about oneself, and thinking only of God. Thinking in this way, the heart remains free, happy, and clear.

Practically speaking, all our own will must be given up to the will of God. We must renounce all our personal desires, however good they seem, and we must want only what is God's will from eternity. We must be indifferent to everything whether for the body, for the soul, or for temporal and eternal things. We must forget the past, leave the future to divine providence, and give the present time to God. We must be content with the present which brings us whatever God has decreed for us and which is an infallible declaration of the will of God. We must never attribute to the self anything that happens to us; but we must consider that everything comes infallibly from His hand, except our own sin.

Let yourself be led to God whichever way pleases Him, either inwardly or outwardly! Do not do like the people who abandon themselves to God for a time, and go back to themselves later on.

You will find comfort only in the love of the cross and in complete yielding. Yielding and the cross go together.

As soon as you would do something which is distasteful to you, yield to God first and it will become less heavy. You will also have to accept all conditions which God may choose to put into your life, choosing none by yourself except staying near Him, loving Him, and yielding to Him, while at the same time receiving all that He gives you, whether it be light or darkness.

What are you afraid of? Why do you not quickly throw yourself in the arms of Love, which were stretched out on the cross only to receive you? What are you risking

3

if you trust God and kneel to Him? Ah! He won't deceive you. Isaiah assures us that we must fear nothing, because He takes special care of us as a mother does her child.

We must yield to the Spirit of God and let ourselves be led by His movements.

The Song of Songs

Concerning Abandonment, here are my words and my meaning in the book I have written on the *Song of Songs*.

The fortresses and the ramparts which protect the believer are constituted in the total yielding of the believer to his God. Trust, faith, hope have strengthened his yielding.

The Bridegroom only wanted to test your fidelity and see whether you were abandoned to His will. The Beloved, in spite of the failings of His Bride, takes her hand and leads her to a small passage which is still open to her, namely yielding. He does this in spite of the aversions which the Bride feels when yielding so completely.

A believer who has achieved this level can submit to every wish of God, and will not refuse Him anything. When God explains His particular plans, He asks for the most extreme renunciations and the greatest sacrifices. Ah! that is when the believer's whole heart is moved, and when he finds misery where he thought none yet existed.

God makes His continual dwelling near the believers who have yielded to Him, near quick and rapid waters which stop for nothing in the world and which, when the slightest obstacle is put in their way, swell with more force and run more impetuously. O, poor ones who fight all your life, you will gather only small victories although they cost you many wounds! If you gave yourselves to God well and truly, and abandoned yourselves to Him, you would be more formidable than an infinite number of men armed for battle.

The greatest waters of afflictions, of contradictions, of miseries, poverty and unhappiness cannot destroy the believer. The streams of abandonment to God likewise will not destroy such a one. If a man has enough courage to give up what he owns and his identity in order to obtain divine Love—which is only acquired when all the rest is lost – he then would never despise what he has attained and turn back away from it.

Are my words different from those of
Thomas A. Kempis

Jesus Christ says that He is the one who fathoms the hearts and knows what every person thinks and desires, as well as the motive of what he desires, and all his intentions. Therefore, leave everything in His care and let Him lead you. If you want to possess Him completely, you must give yourself completely to Him, without keeping anything of yourself to yourself. Abandon yourself completely to Him from the bottom of your heart, with all that you can or wish to possess in this life.

Saint Paul gave up his reputation to God. We can see the bottom of his heart. He used only humility and patience against those who misrepresented him.

Lord, how may times must I abandon myself to You, or in what case must I forget myself?

Christ says that you should always abandon yourself to Him, at every moment, in the least important things as well as in the most important ones. There are no exceptions. He wants to find that in everything you have renounced everything. Always leave in His hands everything that concerns you. He will take care of everything, and He will make everything right in time. Await His orders and His will, and you will obtain great advantage from submitting to Him.

Lord, it is with great joy that I give up to You the care of all that concerns me, because when I want to take care of it myself, I know how I worry needlessly.

Now I turn your attention to the writings of others on the subject of abandonment.

Henri Suso

As the believer advances, there must be a yielding without limits, by which he abandons himself to God everywhere he finds himself, as if he were no longer interested in himself. And God then and there enforces His complete domination over him.

Catherine of Genoa

O blessed is the believer who in everything dies to his own will, because he then lives in God in everything, and God even lives in him! Catherine wanted to die to herself so much that if someone had asked her, "What would you like in heaven or on earth?" she would have said, "Nothing, but I wish to be what I am at this hour and at this moment." We must never want something different from what is happening from one moment to the next, always trying to do God's will.

The love of God operates, as He wishes, through all the activities of such a believer. All the believer's powers are obedient to God, all submitted to Him, and the believer could not wish for anything different. Catherine said: If someone had asked me, "What do you want? What do you understand? What do you remember?" I would have answered: "I want nothing, I understand nothing, and I remember nothing apart from what God in His love wants, understands, and remembers." Since Love has taken care of everything for me and in me, I have not worried about it at all.

Theresa

It is right that the believer should give himself to God and yield to the arms of God. If God wants to take this believer to heaven, he should go. If God should want to take him to hell, he should follow, and he shouldn't worry about it since he walks with God. If God wants to take this person's life, he must be happy about it. If He wants him to live another thousand years, he must agree with the divine will of God. So His Majesty can do with this believer whatever He wants, for the believer does not belong to himself anymore and is not master of his own personality. He is completely given to God.

My Lord, I have nothing; but do not leave me, and I will never give up on You. If all the clerics conspire against me, if all things in creation persecute me, if the devils torment me, I won't care. You mustn't leave me, because I know by experience what advantage can be obtained from suffering by those who trust in You alone.

In order to get to the level we are talking about, God does not want you to keep anything, not a little nor a lot. He wants all without exception or reservation. The believer who has abandoned himself into the hands of God wants nothing except that God should do unto him as He pleases. He remains at peace and allows God to do His will.

Ah! You do not want anything from a believer who has decided to love You and to abandon himself into Your hands. You want nothing but obedience. The believer no longer has to find the way nor to think about what he must do. His will is already Yours.

Francis of Sales

We can, as small children of the heavenly Father, go with Him in two ways: Firstly, we can go, walking by the strength of our own will, always holding with the hand of our obedience to the hand of His divine plan, and following everywhere His plan takes us. For this I must have my own will through which I follow His will, conforming to it.

Secondly, we can go to our Lord without any self-will, simply allowing ourselves to be carried according to His divine will, as a small child in the hands of his mother, wanting no other thing, and simply agreeing to everything that God wants done in us, to us and of us.

We must be like this; we must make ourselves pliable and malleable to God's will, as if we were made of wax. We must not play around at wanting and wishing for things. We must let God do as He wishes and make things happen for us as He so wishes. We accept events, those we like and those we do not, for He will take care of the success of our affairs, and He wants for us what will be best. It is a good thing to leave all our will to God, and He will choose the best way!

To bless God and to thank Him for all the events He so wills is a very holy state. We let God do the willing for us so that He can will and do whatever He wants in us and of us.

The daughter of a very good doctor was having a continual temperature. Knowing that her father only loved her, she said to one of her friends, "I suffer so much; however, I never think of medicines, for I do not know what could cure me. I could wish for one thing, but I would need something else. Therefore, wouldn't it be better for me to leave the choice to my father who does know, who can do, and who wants everything that is good for my health. I would be wrong to think about it; for he will think of it for me. I would be wrong to wish for something, for he will want all that is good for me. I'm waiting for him to do what he will consider good. I will only look to him to show him my love and to let him know that I trust him completely."

Later on her father asked her whether she would mind being weak in order to be

6

cured. "I belong to you, my father," she answered, "I don't know what to wish for in order to be cured. It is you who must wish and do for me all that will seem good to you. As for me, it is enough for me to love you and honor you with all my heart as I am doing." At that point they put a bandage on her arm and her own father opened one of her veins with a lancet. As the blood came out, this lovable young girl never looked at her bleeding arm nor at the blood coming out of the vein, but keeping her eyes on the face of her father, she only said from time to time, "My father loves me and I am all his." When everything was done, she did not thank him, but only repeated the same words of love and trust.

John of Saint Samson

Man can do nothing better than to let himself go and leave everything to God. Such ones are always content and happy, giving themselves totally and with great love into the hands of their infinite God, so that everything would be done to them and in them according to His will. Although it is true that the time and the success vary in them because of His different ways, it does not matter. He is their all, their paradise, because truly they are His!

There is a subtle snag which is the loss of the quietness of the senses through which nobody wants to go. When you yield yourself completely and purely, you do not want to lose the quietness of the senses—although it would be losing without really losing. For if you abandon yourself to Him always and everywhere, you make your quietness simple and of the inner spirit, and you can simply and quietly enjoy God, who is Himself your quietness.

Remember that the holiness of God inside men consists in the entire yielding and resignation of themselves so that they lose themselves in God. Gain and abundance must be replaced by loss and yielding.

Saint Augustine

Let all imagination stop. Let the heavens be silenced. The believer must himself keep in a deep silence. He must yield himself completely to God, as if it he didn't think about faith anymore.

2

ACTION OR INACTION
IN PRAYER

A Short and Simple Method of Prayer

A few people, having heard of the kind of deep silent prayer that I describe, have persuaded themselves wrongly that the believer engaged in silent prayer remains stupid, dead, without acting. But it is certain that he acts there more nobly and more widely than he has ever done up to that time, because he is being moved by God Himself. He is acting through God's Spirit. Saint Paul wants us to let ourselves be moved by the Spirit of God. This is not to say that we must not act, but we must act depending on the movement of God's grace. This action of the believer is a restful action. When the believer acts by himself, he acts with effort. But when he acts in dependence on the Spirit of Grace, his action is so free, so easy, so natural that it does not seem that he is acting. It is an action, so noble, so peaceful, so tranquil that the believer thinks he does not act, because in fact he acts naturally by the Spirit.

When a wheel is scarcely moving, one can see it very well; but when it is going at high speed one cannot distinguish anything about it. In the same way the believer who is resting in God acts in an infinitely noble fashion, but a very peaceful one. The more peaceful he is the faster he moves, because he yields to the Spirit which moves in him and for him. This Spirit is none other than God who attracts us, and who, while pulling us to Himself, makes us run to Him. Therefore, it is not a matter of not doing anything, but of acting in dependence on the Spirit of God. God acting infinitely and we allowing ourselves be moved by the Spirit of God, we act much more than we would by our own actions.

Our actions must consist in making ourselves subject to the action of God and letting the Word imprint His image on us. A canvas which moves would prevent the painter from constituting a painting on it. All the movements which we do by our own spirit prevent this wonderful Painter from doing His work. We must therefore remain peaceful and move only when He moves.

This type of action is clearly more noble. It is certain that these have value only as far as they are noble, grand and uplifting. God's actions are designed; on the other hand, man's actions—however good they seem—are only human actions.

We do not pretend that we do not act, but we only act through our dependence on the Spirit of God, to give His action free reign. This can only be done through the believer's consent. And the believer can only give his agreement by minimizing his own action – to give rise little by little to the actions of God instead.

Jesus Christ shows us this kind of behavior in the Gospel. Martha was doing good things; but because she did them through her human effort, Jesus corrected her. The spirit of man is stormy and unquiet. That is why he achieves little although he may appear to be doing a lot. "Martha," said Jesus, "you worry and try to do many things, but only one thing is necessary. Mary has chosen the better part, and it will not be taken from her." What did she choose? Peace, quietness and repose. It appears that she stopped doing things, to let herself be moved by the Spirit of Jesus Christ.

The actions of man are either exterior or interior. The exterior ones are those which can be seen from outside and concern something that can be touched. The interior actions are the movements of man's spirit. His exterior actions have no value unless they arise from the impulse of the interior action, which is the movement of his spirit. I do not want to speak about the exterior actions, but only of interior actions.

When I want to obey God, but also want to do something that is not of God, I turn away from Him and I turn to something of the world. Then when I want to return to God, I have to take an action to disengage myself from this worldly thing and turn back to God. Until I am perfectly transformed, I need to turn myself often toward God. Some can do it all at once. Others do it little by little. But my action must carry me nearer to God, using all my strength for Him.

The spirit of man is not strong in the beginning, and the believer is used to turning to outward things. He becomes distracted easily and sometimes takes a wrong path. As soon as he notices that he has gotten lost in exterior things, he must, by a simple act of returning to God, go back to Him. The believer continues repeatedly turning back to God in sincerity and simplicity.

Since repeated actions become habits, the believer gets used to living his Christian life, and performing Christian actions becomes customary thereafter. He must not at that point begin to look for such actions to do them. If he gets out of his interior state while he is looking for Christian works to do, he may lose sight of God. One who searches for an action is not keeping his place near to God. He will come back to the heart of God after having been away from Him, but he should stay there quietly as soon as he has reached that place.

It is wrong to believe that we must not act. We always act. We must do actions according to the stage that we have reached.

Even spiritual people find this difficult, so I will try to make it clearer. There are passing and distinct acts. These must be done by people who have turned away from God. They must go back by a distinctive action, according to how far they wandered away from God. Sometimes a very simple action is sufficient. Then there are continuous actions, direct actions, reflex actions. I call a continuous act one by which the believer is turned completely to God through a direct action that does not have to be renewed. Of course it may be interrupted, but it subsists nonetheless. The believer completely turned toward God is in fellowship with Him and remains there in His love. This believer will act as from habit and quietude. This repose is not laziness, for there is action which is a sweet thinking on God, where God is attracting the believer's heart strongly, always more strongly; and the believer is following His strong attraction, remaining in His love, thinking more and more on His love. His actions are stronger and more prompt than all the actions of the person who needs to often return to God.

Now the believer, who is in this deep and strong action of being always turned towards God, does not notice this action because it is simple, direct, and done without thinking about it. The result is that this person does not explain himself very clearly. He *may* say that he is not doing any actions. He *should* say that he cannot distinguish his actions anymore. He does not do them by himself, it is true, but he is attracted to God and follows Him. Love is a weight which drags him down deeper, as a person who falls into the sea and sinks down and would go on sinking forever if the sea were infinite. Without noticing that it was sinking, the weight would go down into the deep at an incredible speed. Thus it is incorrect to say that we do not act.

12

Everyone acts, but everyone does not act in the same way. The error comes from the fact that all those who know they must act would like the actions to be distinct and perceptible. This is not possible if the actions are in spirit.

Physical actions are for beginners; spiritual actions are for those who are more advanced. If we stop at doing the first acts which are weak, we would deprive ourselves of the later ones which are in spirit. Then we would not make much progress. However, we must not try to make the later before we have done the first ones. That would be another kind of misuse.

I further explain my words as written in
The Song of Songs

The return of the Bride is as rapid and sincere as her sin had been light and unforeseen. This beautiful Bride has two qualities like a palm tree: the first, never to curl back on herself, although she has grace from God; the second, not to produce the slightest action by herself, however small it might be.

The Bride invites her Spouse to go everywhere, for she has started doing some action. As God is always acting and is always quiet, in the same way this believer is in perfect quiet inside while acting outwardly.

Others have written as I have written:
Catherine of Genoa

The believer has been taken over by love, though no one would be able to notice, either inwardly or outwardly.

John of the Cross

The Holy Spirit operates in the believer transformed by love. The acts of love of the believer are very precious. The difference which exists between habit and action also exists between transformation into love and the flame of love. It is like the difference between burning wood and the flame. The believer's will is absorbed in the flame of the Holy Spirit. This believer cannot take any action unless the Holy Spirit is pushing him in that direction. The believer is moved by God in this way. It seems to the believer that every time this flames blazes, he has a sense that he is being raised to God.

The Christian who is just beginning to recognize how the Holy Spirit stirs his own spirit will at first be active, be discussing the things of the Spirit, and be praying in an active way too. But later, he will not pray until the Holy Spirit moves in his own spirit and gives him a prayer to pray. If he does not wait to pray the prayer that God gives him, but prays as he formerly did, that would be a distraction from his walk in spirit and his progress toward walking in an interior way. If before, he was looking for desire and fervor and found them, now he must not want either nor look for them. Even if he searched diligently, he would not find either, but on the contrary, he would only get aridity for his search. Now he enjoys the tranquil and quiet peace which is given to him secretly in spirit. This believer must not put his own effort as an obstacle in the way of

God, who is secretly and quietly putting in him wisdom and love. The believer must be concerned only with the attention of a loving God, apart from actions which he feels inclined to do for God. He must remain passive without trying to be diligent.

Many times God anoints the believer with some delicate and loving unction that is quiet, peaceful, solitary, and very far away from the mind or physical senses. Some will come to him like they were banging on a blacksmith's anvil, and speak in this way: "Go on, get out of this, for you are wasting your time and doing nothing. Instead you should take up some different exercise, pray and do something, because you need to act diligently." Such a person does not understand the stages of prayer nor the ways of the spirit. They do not see that these actions they want our believer to do have already been done. When a person walking has reached his goal, he must not go on walking anymore, because it would mean that he would only be moving away from his goal. Action would only take the believer away from his solitude and retreat, and consequently away from the excellent work God had done in him. The actions which are done in this believer's silent prayer are more excellent actions because he is near God and detached from other desires.

The will to go to God will cause us to discard delicious and pleasurable things rather than to hold onto them. By that we fulfill the rule of love, which is to love God above all things. This can be accomplished, but it requires the believer's nakedness and being empty of all things. God has taken great pains to lead the believer to this point, and He highly values the fact that He has led him into solitude, so that He can talk to his heart (which is what He always wants to do). He is the one who rules the heart of the believer with an abundance of peace and quiet, and puts a stop to human effort, with which even "working all night they achieve nothing."

James of Jesus

The aim of the believer who is walking this path is to be essentially annihilated and consumed by divine light so that he neither feels, loves, desires, nor rejoices in anything other than in God alone. This is with such serenity that he does not labor for anything. This loving and simple affection is intimate and innate to the believer at this stage in his progress. This process seems to belong to his spirit and not to his abilities. This is partly because of the inner and deep roots of his love for God and partly because of the simplicity and sweetness of God, whose perfection is nearer to quietness than it is to movement. What the believer does now is more like a habit than an action, because this believer is now usually inclined to love God. Habitual inclination toward God makes what is an action seem not to be one. It is a part of reality and transformation of being. The reason for this is that action is movement, and exercise of the spirit may last for only moments. The believer does not feel himself move, but rather, in this divine affection he senses a kind of immutability of continuance that does not seem to be an action, but rather a condition of being moved in a preordered fashion.

Francis of Sales

When you are in this pure, simple, filial trust with our Lord, stay there without leaving at all to do acts of the senses. Do no acts from the mind, nor from the will, for this simple and trusting love and this loving lethargy of your spirit in the arms of your Savior comprises all you ever thought of. It is better to sleep on His sacred chest than to be awake somewhere else, wherever it might be.

John of Saint Samson

We speak here and elsewhere that in this noble, deep and active plunge, the believer is not without action nor without some kinds of formulated thought. But in this place, the believer's action is done so subtly that one can say he can hardly sense the actions himself. He is not unaware of his action, for his action is always done with a simple, avid and hungry desire to possess his beloved Lord, without dissimilitude, and not for his own satisfaction, but for God's.

The believer is not sufficiently disposed nor prepared to enter the higher life of the spirit if he has not abandoned his power of doing, in exchange for the simplicity and purity of this mystical way. God from now on acts and works in such a believer's deeds as He pleases. The believer is rightly and willingly the living tool of our Lord, who likes to perfect His work in him. Thus God makes him worthy of having the Holy Spirit reside in his spirit and live his life for him—at least as completely as it is possible while living on this earth.

I now turn your attention to the book entitled
The Mystical Day

God is the only being of faith. He only can operate both in Himself and outside Himself. In His believers He can do what He wishes, giving them freely the state of being, and giving them freedom. The believer's action, therefore, is more the being and the action of God than it is of the believer himself.

The believer rests in God, who remains hidden from the believer. God's actions cannot be noticed or reflected through intuitive or formal knowledge.

In silent worship and silent prayer Love works. Getting to the innermost part of the believer, God changes the believer's life into that of the life of the Beloved, so that he wants only what God wants and he wants everything that God wants.

The mystical action of the prayer of repose is more uniting and transforming. There are several different degrees of uniting love, several sorts of divine unions. One is done through acts of mystical love, and is so intimate and so immediate that among all others it seems the only one to be desired absolutely.

Perfect union will be characterized by actual and faithful connection to God's Spirit, to follow in prayer the inclination toward God. This may be either by taking action where it is needed for the upkeep and the maintenance of prayer, or by voluntarily giving up those very actions when it pleases God to give a kind of quietness inconsistent with the believer's will. Too much eagerness to produce good acts, when God wants you to defer them to His sweet dealings in the inner part of your spirit, is detrimental to your progress.

When you are in a quiet stage of prayer that is focused on some glimpsed truth, you have not abandoned action, because the energy in your quiet prayer is action of spirit. But when you are in a state of obscure worship, in which you do not know what the Lord would have you focus on, then you give up all action to stay in a state of mystical quietness, which is really a state of consent or love or surrender. In this prayer of delectable quietness there is no desire to act nor to change to some other type of prayer. In this enjoyable condition you feel a delightful inner touch which prevents you from any other type of prayer, and this quietness suspends any other inner act.

Then do not worry and force yourself to produce acts that are unnatural. Endure with a cheerful heart the fact that God deprives you of such accomplishments, so that in this interior poverty you may enter the real poverty of spirit. Those who want always to be doing some action without training themselves for the prayer of repose will never achieve this poverty of mind and will never be able to reach the poverty in spirit that our Lord so often spoke of. It is this which the mystics mention so often, and it consists in the fact that the believer does not own his own acts and his own satisfaction in prayer.

It is not easy to give up active praying, even when the Lord may be leading us into more silent worship. God must do this for us. (If we give up active praying for silent worship when it is not God doing it in us, then the natural tendency will be to give up praying altogether. The result would be a spiritual void and great vulnerability.)

3

GIVING OUR WILL
TO
GOD'S WILL

I turn your attention to my book,
A Short and Simple Way to Pray

This is what I have said in *A Short and Simple Way to Pray.* Are my words different from devout Christians who have come before me?

The believer must let himself be destroyed by the strength of Love. How do we get into God? It can be done only by getting out of ourselves in order to lose ourselves within Him. This will never happen unless we annihilate ourselves.

The believer is put face-to-face with the wholeness of God and the nothingness of man. We can only honor the wholeness of God by annihilating ourselves. We are no sooner annihilated than God, who cannot endure emptiness without filling it, fills us with Himself.

The knowledge of our nothingness helps us to know the wholeness of God. It is in the wholeness of God that we can draw the necessary light to discover the nothingness of man.

Annihilation of the self is a very necessary stage. If you want God to become alive in you, you must have reached the last stage of nothingness. The fruits of annihilation can be seen there. The believer, being annihilated, has such respect and obedience for the grace of God that he does not disdain nor reject divine visitation . . . or comfort.

The attributes of God are valiant soldiers who guard the royal couch and prevent from entering those who are not completely annihilated. The Bridegroom calls the believer His Bride, and He urges her to hurry and let herself be destroyed and annihilated.

The Bride stays in the arms of her Spouse as though she does not exist. This is the result of the deepest annihilation.

Now, here is what other authors have said concerning the devastation of sacrificing our will to God's will. Once more I ask, are my words different from those who lived before us?
nothingness, or whether he is human, or whether he has reached unity. As soon as he notices that he is experiencing nothingness, he may draw away from it and reflect upon his natural consciousness of self. When someone is so much in spirit that he knows neither himself nor anything else, but is all sleepy in eternal nothingness, then he is completely lost in God.

Thomas A. Kempis

If I lose all feelings about myself, if I make myself the lowest of the low, if I annihilate myself, if I reduce myself to ashes and dust, as I know I am, Your grace will be favorable to me and Your light will shine in my heart.

Henri Harphius

This light reveals the nature of nothingness, the sublimity of which forces man to put an end to all action, as he is overcome by the action of divine love.

Catherine of Genoa

When a believer is annihilated, he does not act any more, he does not speak anymore, he does not wish for anything anymore, he has no feelings inside or out which could move him. In everything God rules him and leads him.

It is God who annihilates the believer. God alone remains; and the believer remains as though he had no soul. God gives him intelligence as He likes.

Oh, if I could only speak and say what I know and what I feel about this annihilation of the will, I am sure that each of us would hate his own will as much as he hates the devil!

God gives the believer some inner occupation in which he keeps him so much absorbed that it seems to the believer that he is plunged into a deep sea, being fascinated by so great and so divine a reality that he cannot do ordinary things. But remaining annihilated and plunged into this sea, he receives so much divine peace that it could sweeten hell.

When the believer finds himself annihilated through divine intervention, he is transformed within God, who leads him and moves him in His own way without human intervention. Imagine what this person would say if he could talk about it. His words would be so inflamed that hearts would be afire. In this annihilation the believer knows that all wishes are painful, all intelligence is boring, all memory is hindrance.

This is what God does to man, who was created in order to be united to God and transformed in Him. When we eat bread, it is divided into two substances. One part nourishes us and the other part is eliminated as superfluous. In like manner God separates from man the instincts that are corrupted by original sin, which would incline him to every kind of evil. The believer, feeling that dangerous condition, says "I have no remedy for this apart from the fact that God should do unto me as I do with bread. When I have eaten it, my constitution keeps only the good substance and casts the rest out. In this way I am fed and healthy."

If God with His sweet ways did not work in us marvelous things, we would never let ourselves be annihilated. We would fight as much as we could. But we find ourselves in accord with the arrangements of God, and God cuts away little by little as if pruning a tree. We begin to realize that we can have no pleasure in the material things and find nothing good unless we happily let God deal with us as He wishes.

John of the Cross

"I have been reduced to nothingness," says David, "and I didn't even know it." This believer does not know where he is going. He finds himself annihilated for all the things he used to savor, things from above and things from here below. He finds himself in love with Love without knowing how.

Benoit of Canfield

There are two kinds of annihilation, the active kind and the passive kind. The passive kind occurs when the person and everything is annihilated, is asleep, has fainted. Passive annihilation occurs when no feelings and no physical image remain. The passive annihilation exists in the spirit, and consists in true knowledge of God Himself, though all of this is not necessarily based on experience. The active annihilation occurs when there is still some image or feeling, although the person knows that he is nothing. One kind is consciously experienced, the believer seeing himself reduced to nothing. As it is written, "I am reduced to nothing."

Of these two kinds of annihilation, the active one is the more perfect because it annihilates everything along with oneself. God annihilates the believer and all things that remain, or even when they do not remain, and even when the believer faints. God even annihilates what annihilates all things: that is to say, the believer's intelligence, knowledge, and abilities. He does not let any feeling or image remain, but God alone. Active annihilation is more perfect in its strength because no external worries nor multiple intellectual acts are able to prevent this annihilation, nor distract from it. He annihilates things not only when the believer is raised above himself, but also when he is recollected into himself. In this way active annihilation continues and envelops everything.

John of Saint Samson

For those who are really dead, I say that it is infinitely better to be completely annihilated than to be completely dead; for death is the entry to annihilation. Now what and whom are we talking about? Since so few find themselves completely dead, what we are saying really does not matter. Those who are completely annihilated, according to the last and highest stage, remain from then on even more unknown and ignored because they are different from other mystics.

Passive annihilation occurs when, either inside or outside, there is no other activity but to look at God and worship Him in purity and silence. Such a state is very properly called passive, because during all that time the believer is the recipient of divine action, which is a passive state even though he experiences it strongly and joyfully. He is spiritually passive. On the contrary, active annihilation occurs when all that we have to do seems to us to be nothing, and as if it had never existed.

Since God has deigned to take pleasure in our annihilation and since in this way He has satisfied His love, we must, in order to satisfy Him, remain annihilated to all things, pertaining both to Him and to us. We must pay attention to our reflections which are nothing and do nothing for us, because we are being transfused entirely and perfectly in the whole range of God, in which "we are, we move, and live of the same divine life," and which is the cause of our experiencing heaven here below.

Renunciation of self must be practiced if it is to be deep and subtle, which it must be, so that it may become stable, producing the same effect in the believer's life at all times. This pure, simple and subtle renunciation consists of being entirely lost to oneself in a state of powerlessness, in a state where one wishes for nothing, where one does not live but is not dead. This is a state where the individual is not allowed to look after

21

himself in even the smallest way. This is easy to say, but to practice this sort of thing seems impossible. Could believers be found who are faithful enough to their Bridegroom to remain in their innermost being, forever unknown to man, while they are enduring being tested? Believers who do keep looking inward to Christ become constant and eventually will be forever lost in the abundance of the ineffable joy of God in Whom they have completely engulfed themselves.

4

CENTERING

A Short and Simple Way to Pray

Living faith in God, who is present in our hearts, must incline us to go deeply into ourselves, gathering all our outward senses and drawing them into our inner self, thus preventing them from being scattered. This is a great way to get rid of many distracting things from the start, and of going away from the exterior world to get nearer to God. He can be found only in our inner selves and in the center of our being, which is the "holy of holies" where He lives.

This way of turning toward Him is very easy and makes the believer progress effortlessly and quite naturally, because God is his center. The center of a thing always attracts very strongly. The more your center is turned toward spiritual things, the more it attracts very strongly, bringing outward things inward. And its attraction cannot be stopped.

As soon as one is turned toward one's center, unless he is stopped by some invincible obstacle, he rushes toward the center at a very great speed. As soon as a stone is thrown in the air and turns toward the earth, it is attracted downward by its own weight as toward its center. The same is true of water or fire, which, if they are not stopped, run incessantly toward their center.

So I say that the believer, because of the effort he has made to gather to his center, and since he is inclined toward his center without any other incentive but the weight of love, he does fold gradually toward the center. The more he remains peaceful and quiet without moving, the more he advances speedily because of the power of that central attraction which strongly pulls him towards the center. As soon as he is on that central incline, that is to say, turning inward through silent prayer and worship, from that very moment he is acting very strongly. He is rushing toward his center which is attracting him, and this speed is much greater than any action could be. Nothing equals the speed of the incline toward the center.

When the believer is turned toward his inner self in the way described, he is on an incline toward the center, and he wishes strongly to be united with God. This tendency is the beginning. Later on when he comes nearer and nearer to God he is finally united to Him. Then they become one, which is to become one spirit with Him. It is then that this spirit which came from God goes back to its beginning.

I point you also to my work found in
The Song of Songs

Enjoying God is permanent and lasting because it is in our innermost being. Because God is our final purpose, we can always let ourselves go into Him, for God is our ultimate purpose and our center. Thus we can let ourselves be merged in Him and transformed.

We must also note that when God created us He gave us a part of His own being so that we could be reunited with Him through that spiritual part of us. At the same time, He gave us a tendency toward this unity. If we think of man in the state of innocence before the Fall, then we can see that He has given something of Himself to man in his

25

human body that causes him to have a tendency to unite with God who is his origin.

The young Bride prays to her Spouse to draw her toward Him through the center of her being, which is her spirit, as if she was not sure of her own powers. She already lives by the grace of her Spouse and He continues to attract her strongly to delight in Him more nobly and more intimately than she presently does. This is what incites her to ask from her Spouse. She says, "Drag me into the most intimate part of my inner self so that my powers and my senses rush toward You in a deeper but less sensuous way. Drag me," she says, "Oh my divine Lover."

We rush to You through this very personal worship which makes us feel Your divine might through which You attract us to Yourself. We run following a kind of aroma which Your attraction makes us sense. We will go beyond this aroma to get to You Yourself, as You are the center of our happiness.

The Lord is still in the innermost part of the believer who is faithful to Him. However, He often remains so hidden that the believer, who has reached this stage of happiness, usually does not know about it except in some moments when God chooses to manifest Himself to him. The believer then discovers Him in deep and strong experience.

The Bride says, "When my King was in His bed . . . . " The one who leads me and governs me is my King and His bed is the innermost part of my being where He takes His rest. My faithfulness "has given out its aroma" in such a sweet and pleasant way that He had to make it known to me. Then I knew that He was taking His repose in me as in His royal bed. I had known nothing of His presence there before, for although He was there I did not perceive His presence.

The Bridegroom kisses His lover, and He is in her. He embraces her from the outside, and He moves into her deepest being. She feels that in mystical sleep He goes ever deeper into her being. He unites Himself to her, not only as before, through the powers which are referred to as "hills"; but even more, going beyond the hills He comes to the top of the "mountain" which is the center. There He really touches her and unites Himself to her. She feels that His touch is very different from any former power, and that affects her greatly even though it is a passing touch which is not yet a permanent and lasting union.

We must go beyond all things to go into the bosom of the Father, to repose there without any moderation, losing everything. Immediate and central union can only happen outside of all created things.

The instinct that pushes the believer towards his God who is limitless cannot be compared to the physical instinct towards earthly things which are finite. When the believer's instinct pushes him towards God, his spirit is not hampered. There is nothing that has such vehemence and such impulsiveness as this desire for God.

I turn your attention to:
John of the Cross

The work of the Holy Spirit takes place in the believer's spirit, the deepest place, where neither the world nor the devil nor the believer's own physical senses can touch. The more interior this experience is and the more free from bodily senses, the purer it is. And the purer it is, the more often and more abundantly God communicates with the believer. Since the believer's spirit is very free and very separate, all of the spirit's occupation is to receive God. It is only in the spirit of the believer that God moves to work in him without the employment of the outward senses. Thus all the movements of this indwelt spirit are divine. Although they are from God, they are also from the believer's spirit because God lives there and works there. The believer contributes only by his willing consent. When we say that God strikes at the deepest part of the believer, it must mean that the believer has other centers which are not so deep. We shall try to see how all this happens.

We call the center the deepest place which anything can reach. This part no longer has the strength and ability to move. It can go no further. Let us follow this idea. A stone when it is in the earth is as if it is in its own center, because it is in the sphere of its activity and motion; but it is not at the deepest part of the earth. It still has strength enough to go down to center of the earth if the impediments preventing it are taken away. When the stone reaches the center of the earth where it will no longer have the power to move, then we say that it is at the deepest, at the center.

Now God is the center. Reaching the center, the believer will have gotten to his last and deepest stage. This will happen when with all his strength he loves, understands and enjoys God. He has not reached that stage if he has enough strength and ability to go further – although he is in God through grace and redemption. If this is the case he must not be satisfied. Although he is in God, he is not at the deepest stage since he could go further. Love unites the believer's heart with God, and the more stages of love he gets to, the further and deeper he will unite with God.

Francis of Sales

In some cases union with God comes not through repeated transports, but in continual gradual steps when the heart becomes aware of the goodness of God. A great weight such as iron or stone goes deeper and presses so much against the earth on which it stands, even though it is not being pushed, that in time it becomes completely buried because of its own weight. Its weight tends to push it to the center. It is the same way with our heart, once it has been united with God. If it remains united with Him for some time, and if nothing comes between our heart and God, we will continue to go deeper by an inexorable progress of union until we are completely with God. This is because of the inclination which His love gives us to unite evermore to His almighty goodness.

Friar John of Saint Samson

It is a very strange thing that men do not know the stages and the proper exercises for reaching their infinite happiness. They never know what is in their inner self, nor do they know God's loving devotion to them. But when a man gets to his center, then he takes his rest in God with great pleasure. Enjoying God occupies him completely with delight in a very subtle, very simple, and very spiritual fashion, which is most often above himself and above all physical senses and all perception. While he remains in this stage, he is very far from sensing any loss. On the other hand, when he is occupied with *thoughts about* God he is far from this center.

All the stages which precede this one are mentioned by the mystics, but this one contains all the other stages in a divine way. By this way one feels melted and reduced to a very small point, which is the one and only center from whence all the lines which can be conceived are drawn. What is constituted under feeling, and simple or specific perception, seems to show the human side of us in a very excellent way more than it reveals the Uncreated where we do not exist. This Uncreated keeps us caught above all love in unique nakedness and simplicity, and is very essential. Previously there was mention of divine fire which inflamed and consumed the believer with faith. What we are talking about now is higher than that. The believer who has reached this point cannot find any words or any thoughts to express what he has seen or felt in the preceding stages, much less in the stage that he has now reached.

Monsignor Olier

The Spouse, at last meeting the Bride, gives Himself to her. Because He loves her so much, He gives her power over Him, saying to His dear Bride what He used to say to God His Father: "All I have is Yours, all You have is Mine." So He is everything for the Bride, as the Bride is everything for Him. The Bride must then remain peaceful in her inner self, living always obedient to the commands of her Spouse and always ready to answer faithfully His wishes.

Now we turn to the author of
The Mystical Day

In this kind of prayer the believer remains silent in God through love rather than through knowledge. Heavy things tend toward their center without knowing that there is an attraction emanating from the center. Iron is attracted by the magnet without knowing that there is a law of attraction between them. The same thing happens to the believer without his knowing why, when he remains quiet. The human spirit is the most noble power in the believer's inner being. The spirit is the part of the believer which has in its most intimate inner center the real presence of God. Taulere says that the Trinity shines in the inner self and spreads intimately in the center, which has neither name nor representation. In this inner self the believer's spirit finds itself shapeless as though lost in the immensity of God. If ever, he also says, we want to reach the inner part of God, we must first get to our own inner self with pure humility. In other places he calls it the inner part of divinity, the eternal innermost part. The most noble part within the believer, he says, lies quietly in the innermost part of divinity, from whence it comes. The one who never looks at or appreciates his innermost part will never communicate with the Eternal One.

The marriage of God with the believer takes place at the center. Abstraction, solitude, and serious application to the inner self are needed for those who desire to reach quietness. When they disengage themselves from outer exercises, they must withdraw to the inner self, and with their senses and everything that is in them turn their thoughts to God, to unite with Him and to lose themselves in the furthest corner of their inmost being. The dignity of such believers cannot be conceived of nor explained.

The innermost part of the believer is his spirit, which has the ability to turn completely to God. Saint Theresa says that God does not care whether we open the doors of our innermost being for Him to enter. She says that the cellar is the innermost part of our being. We cannot enter it by our own efforts. God must lead us to it and God wants nothing from us apart from complete submission of our wills. Without opening any door, God enters the center of our being in the way that Christ entered the room where His disciples were, without going through any door of that room.

Saint Theresa, talking of the union created by God in the believer's spirit, says that in that state the believer benefits enormously because God can act in him without any physical body hindering Him. Not even the believer himself can hinder because God is more the master of the believer than the believer is himself. What we wish for believers is that they must go toward their goal and that they should take the shortest and easiest path.

I have written that it is very simple and easy to come to God. Others have written the same:

Theresa

Although we are only at the beginning of our journey and are still very simple, let us try to think nothing except to incite ourselves to love. If our Lord gives us this grace, this love must engrave itself in our hearts. Then all things will be easy for us, and we will be able to do much in a short time without any effort.

Friar John of Saint Samson

God is for Himself and for you. The shortest and surest way for you to make progress toward Him is to stay in spirit, which is a pure and unique place to be.

5

PASSAGES

Nicholas of Jesus-Maria

This man, Nicholas, extensively quotes many Roman Catholics who have been sainted by the Church. Here are some quotes he has given us of Christians who have come before us.

Every new disciple progresses by stages in the perfection of this science, that is, mysticism. He first exercises with studying and applying his energies to living a moral life. This is a childish way used by beginners. After some time, perhaps a month or two, if he receives some light from God, he should begin to progress to love through silent prayer and worship. It may seem presumptuous to some people that a believer still so full of sin should ask Jesus Christ for a union in love. Saint Theresa said, "If a young disciple does all that he possibly can to detach himself from earthly things, and if he thinks and talks only of his Lord, I believe that there is no doubt that God will give him progress quickly—if he turns his mind completely to Him, as a few saints have done."

The one who has requested me to write this progressed further in four months by the help of our Lord than I did in seventeen years. In a very short time he acquired a great experience in spiritual things. These are gifts which God gives when He wants to and in whatever way He wants to, without consideration of time nor of service. I do not say that time and service are not useful, but often our Lord does not give to one, in a span of twenty years, the progress that He might give to another in one year.

One may think that to proceed from one of these stages to the other it is necessary to have remained a long time in the preceding stage. Although usually it is necessary to have passed through the stages that we have been describing, it is not an irrevocable rule, as you have often been told. As with goods that belong to Him, our Lord gives these graces as He pleases, unto whomever He wishes, and He deprives nobody of something that was their own possession. Saint Gregory has said that the grace of this silent and personal worship is not given to higher people and refused to lower ones. He gives often to the higher ones and often to the lower ones. We must not put any limit nor measure to such a great Lord who wishes so much to grant His favors.

Mark the words of Nicholas of Jesus-Maria: From all these things we must see and admit that human effort is the wrong way to go and that it prevents spiritual progress of believers. People are wrong if, without authority and good reason, they disapprove of this silent and personal prayer and worship which some have experienced even though they do not have a history of studying prayer. They even may still have some taint of imperfections; however, this grace is not granted only to perfect men or to those who have practiced this kind of worship for a long time. John of the Cross has stated that long delay and great perfection are not always required. Often enough all this can be done in a short time.

6

GOD DWELLING
IN US

Here is what I have said in
A Short and Simple Way to Pray

The believer must learn a basic truth: The kingdom of God is in him, and that is where he must look for it. He should understand that God who is inside him deigns to be his Father.

The believer by the way of silent prayer turns toward his inner self to attend to God who is present there. If he turns all his vigor and strength toward his inner self, in so doing he draws away from his physical senses, and those physical senses are left without strength. The more the believer progresses and gets nearer to God the more he leaves himself behind.

The believer finds that God is more inside him than he is himself. He has only one thing to do to find God, namely, to go deeper into himself, and there in prayer he will find Him.

The kingdom of God is inside us. This kingdom can be understood in two ways: First, when God is so much our master that nothing resists Him any longer, then our inner self is really His kingdom. Second, possessing God, we possess the kingdom of God. This is our ultimate happiness, the reason for which we have been created. To serve God is to reign.

The Song of Songs

I did not look after my vine, which is my inner self, where my God resides. Then I realized that He was resting in me as in His royal bed. I did not know this before for, although He was there, I didn't see Him.

Jesus Christ makes Himself a throne in the believer's heart, which He decorates magnificently to make it the place where He resides. There He reigns supremely, for He has obtained the believer's heart with His blood, and He sanctifies it by His own work. God reigns in Jesus Christ and Jesus Christ reigns in pure hearts where he finds no resistance and nothing to displease Him. Here He prepares us for His kingdom and for participation in His kingship. In the same way His Father had prepared His kingdom for Him and had made Him to participate in His Father's kingship. This throne of the King of Kings is made of Lebanese trees. It is the inner self of man, which serves as foundation for the spiritual structure.

Have others written similarly?

Thomas A. Kempis

"The kingdom of God is within you," says the Lord. Turn to it with all your heart and leave this miserable world, and your heart will find peace. Learn to have nothing but contempt for all exterior things and apply yourself only to inner things. You will then see that the kingdom of God will come to you. For the kingdom of God is the peace and joy that you feel with the Holy Spiri—tand this is not given to sinners.

Jesus Christ will come to you and will make you feel the sweetness of His solace, if you prepare in your inner self a residence worthy of Him. All glory and beauty, loved by this heavenly Spouse, is inside the believer's spirit; that is where He takes His delights.

To follow God inside oneself and to have no link and no love for all that is outside is the proper state to be in for a spiritual man.

Theresa

Saint Augustine says that he was looking for God in various places and that he found Him inside himself. It is an important thing for you (who can be so easily distracted and diverted) to listen to this truth and to realize that you do not need to go to heaven to talk to your eternal Father and enjoy Him and comfort yourself in Him. Nor do you need to shout loudly! God is so near us that however softly we speak to Him, He will hear us. The believer does not need wings to find God. He needs only to be alone and to look at God inside himself.

A follower of Saint Augustine said, "Oh, God, where did I direct my quest. Infinite Beauty, I was looking for You outside, and You were in the middle of my heart!"

Albert the Great: Do not worry very much about actual devotion and about the sweetness of the senses or of the tears, but only be united with God in spirit in your inner self.

7

RELAPSES INTO OLD WAYS

The Song of Songs

A person who has given his heart to Jesus Christ is then united with God. Even so a young believer just starting on the way with Christ may be still feeble and may experience eclipses, relapses, may still fall at times. His union with God is confirmed in love. He still remains in God, and he who is in God remains in love, for God is love.

This believer is not so well established in his experience with the Lord that he cannot still look at himself. Being truly unfaithful is relatively rare, and it only comes from weakness. The Spouse has allowed His Bride such small error in order to let her see the damage which can be done when she takes her eyes off of Him to look at herself. This will have value to her in the future as she advances to higher stages of her walk. For the moment she has retreated into herself with ostensibly the best reason in the world— in order to look at the fruit of having lost herself in God, that is, to see whether the vine is flowering, if it is bearing fruit. Does that not seem right and very reasonable? Reasonable, yes, but erroneous.

I turn your attention to what another has said concerning relapses.

Friar John of Saint Samson

Christians are not beyond falling, whether they be beginners, learners, or even those who have reached a very high stage of advancement. On the contrary, I say that the Bridegroom takes great pleasure to exercise believers in various ways through falls that are not severe, but part of common weakness. He prefers that they fall, not because He likes to see them fall, but because a consequence of falling is extreme humility, abnegation, uprightness, and growing stability in the simple and loving union with Him. We must believe that He would never allow them to fall if not to gain these consequences. God wishes only His glory, and He wants to be completely satisfied in all these cases of the renunciation and abnegation of His own, in order that those who arise from their falls still love Him as much as if they had never fallen. Perhaps they love Him even more— even if sometimes they might fall several times in a day.

8

COMMUNICATION AND FELLOWSHIP

There are two kinds of communication. One is the fellowship of God with the believer, and the other is fellowship between Christians. I have written about the second one in other places. During fellowship with God a communication takes place deep inside the believer which is not interrupted by outside events. The believer feels at such times that God is more in him than he is in himself.

Here are some things I said on this topic in
The Song of Songs

Fellowship between the Word of God and the believer comes out of the union of the believer with his Lord. From this union comes fruitfulness. Fruitfulness is given to the believer now made one with God, and the believer progresses in stages until his lips are like honey which distills continually for the benefit of others. It is only his lips, not his word, because it is the Bridegroom who talks through the Bride, and the lips of His Bride are used to express His divine word.

Oh, incomparable Bride, shall I say it? You are one with the very holy Trinity since you receive continuously and you continually give back what you receive.

She brims over with delights because she is full of them to the point of overflowing—as full as a basin full of water which overflows on all sides—so that others can have part of her blessing.

God also invites her to talk to others about inner things, and to teach them what they must do in order to grow in Him. It is one of the main functions of the Bride to teach inner things to friends of the Bridegroom. At that stage the believer is more able than ever to help others.

Once more turn your attention to other authors concerning
Fellowship Between God and the Believer

John of the Cross

Keep this secret between us, that is to say, do not say anything as you used to before when fellowship between us was of the sort that you could communicate to the outer senses. Then people were able to cope with the experiences you would share because they were not so high and so deep, so that the mind could understand them. But now these spiritual mysteries that I speak to you are so sublime, so substantial and so intimate that I must ask you not to say any more about them to people. This is because spiritual substance cannot be communicated to the senses, and thus what can be received by the senses is not essentially God. The believer who wishes for the essential fellowship with God, a communication which does not speak to the senses, asks God that it remain a secret, that is to say, they must not communicate in such a low and exterior way that the physical senses can have any part of it.

The ability which the believer asks for, to love perfectly, is called here "breath of the wind." It is a very delicate touch and sentiment which the believer's spirit feels when communicating with Holy Spirit who wishes to make the believer go further, as the believer also aspires to do. This love, which is delivered by the Holy Spirit, makes the believer progress and teaches him to aspire by wishing to love God. This aspiration is similar to the Father aspiring to the Son and the Son to the Father. It is the Holy Spirit who transforms the believer. It would not be a real transformation, however, if the believer did not change and unite with the Holy Spirit. (This transformation is not of a very high stage, by eternal measure, because of the baseness and depravity of this earthly life.) For the believer, however, it is a very great glory and pleasure—so great that no mortal tongue could express it nor could any human mind understand. God, being in him wants him to progress as God has shown him.

This is what Saint Paul, the way I understand it, meant when he said, "Since you are children of God, God has sent the Spirit of His Son into your hearts, shouting Abba Pater." This is what happens to people who have reached perfection in the way described above, and we should not marvel at the fact that the believer is able to reach such a high stage. Since God gives us His favor, that is to become like Him and unite with Him in the very Holy Trinity, why should it be incredible that a believer should continue his work of comprehension and of love, united in the Trinity. We know that all this happens, and no power nor wisdom is able to explain it. The Son of God has obtained and gained for us this very high and sublime stage.

According to Saint John, Christ said to His Father, "Father, those You have given to Me, I want that wherever I am they must be with Me." So we are participating in the same work that the Father and Son do. He added: "I do not pray only for them" (speaking of those who were then present), "but also for those who will believe in Me. They must be one, united in the same way as You, My Father, live in Me and I in You. They also must be united in Us, so that the world may believe that You have sent Me. I gave them the light that You have given Me, so that they may be united as We are, I in them and they in Me, so that they may be perfectly united and that the world would realize that You have sent Me, and that You have loved them as You have loved Me."

He means to give them the same love that God gives to the Son. We reach, by participation, what He possesses by nature. We participate in His life by union with Him.

God gives light to those who have surrendered to Him. This light is like glass through which the rays of sun shine. Here it is in an even more beautiful state, because the human spirit is intertwined with the Divine Spirit.

Depending on the degree of excellence which unites the human spirit with the divine will, the believer gives to God in God the same goodness he received; for he receives it in order to give it back. And in the same way, according to the degree of progress, a believer who knows the greatness of God, being united with Him, shines and gives out warmth and love. Other divine attributes given to the believer, according to his stage of growth, are strength, excellence, beauty, justice, et cetera. The believer receives these gifts, and he gives them back to his Lord. He gives back the same light that he receives from Him, because he is one with Him. He is in participation with God. Although this process will only happen perfectly in the next life, it is now a shadow of God. In this way, being a shadow of God (because of this transformation), the believer does what God does in him. Thus, in the same way as God gives Himself to the believer freely and graciously, it is as if the believer gives God back to God.

James of Jesus

says:

Let us explain these words of John of the Cross: There are, between God and the believer, divine, intimate and secret communications. They become part of the substance of the believer and are like substantial touches of the divine union. When God sanctifies the believer more than the virtues and gifts, and more than the habitual grace which settles in the essence of the inner man, the person of the Holy Spirit also comes in. In this gift one gets the Holy Spirit and He remains in man.

Henri Suso

(describing believers in an advanced state)

The love and grace of advanced believers is so immense that it rebounds from them onto others, although the others do not know it and do not even want to know it. There are very few such advanced spirits, but God allows His church to be founded on them as on so many pillars. They have given themselves up to God so purely, so nakedly and so simply in their faith that the graces they receive from God cause them more suffering than joy. They desire nothing more than to follow in all simplicity the example of Jesus Christ. They do not wish love, neither wait for any comfort. They are so humble that they deem themselves unworthy of the gifts and the joys or the comforts of God, and they do not even dare want them. Whatever happens to them or to others is always pleasing to them. If God gives them something, they are happy. If God takes it from them, they are equally happy. They take nothing from what is given to them. They do not care for their interests, neither in time nor in eternity. They have abandoned themselves, and they live in an enlightened ignorance, wishing to know nothing. Sometimes it seems that everyone torments them, and they are always ready to suffer and to continue in this way to their last breath. The world does not know them, but they know the world perfectly. They are true worshipers who adore the Father in spirit and in truth.

Catherine of Genoa

This great Christian, lost in the sea of God her Love, would have wanted—if she had been capable of any wish—to communicate to her spiritual children the feelings she had for her sweet Love by which she was overwhelmed. She used to say to them, "Oh, if I could only tell you what my heart feels, that I feel myself burning inside! I can't find the right word to use for such a great love. All that I would say about it would be so unlike it that it would be an insult to this sweet Love. What I can say to you about it is that if the smallest drop of what I feel were in hell, it would become heaven; and there would be such great love and such great unity that the devils would become holy angels, because where God's love is, no pain can survive." A friar who was present at the time said to her, "I do not understand this, but I wish it were possible to understand it better." She answered, "My son, I cannot possibly tell you any more." He answered back, "Mother, if our interpretation was right, would you tell us?" She answered, "Oh, my son, willingly." He then said to her, "I believe that the consequence of the love you feel is a deep and unifying warmth which unites the believer's spirit with God its Love, and which unites it so much with Him through the participation in His goodness, that it cannot be discerned from God. This union is so admirable that there are no words to express it, and one cannot feel, nor taste, nor wish any other thing." She responded, "My dear son, it is really as you have said." The friar said to her, "Ah, mother, can't you ask

God your Love a few drops for your children?" She answered with great joy, "This sweet Love is such that I cannot ask Him anything. All I can do is introduce Him to them."

Theresa

What power is available to believers whom our Lord has led up to this level? Such a believer looks at everything without being part of or wrapped up in things. What shame he or she feels to have wasted time on such thoughts! How astonished these persons are at their former blindness! And what pity they feel for those who are still blind, especially if they are men of prayer, to whom God grants some gifts! These believers would like to shout loudly to them so that they would understand that they have been seduced by false allurement and delights. Sometimes they even do tell them—and afterwards thousands of persecutions attack them. People accuse them of having no humility and wanting to teach those from whom they actually should learn. If this person happens to be a woman, she is condemned unreasonably, because her accusers do not know what force moves her. What truly does move her is such that it cannot be contained, and she cannot help trying to prevent those she loves from falling into error. She wishes to see people free from the prison of this life, which she feels is no less, and indeed it seems to her to be as hard, as if she were to see herself a prisoner.

Oh, my Lord, You got me to a stage where I could have shouted on the rooftop! I know they would not believe me, for they do not believe several others who know how to say it in another way than I say it.

These flowers, at this height, are different and produce a different odor from those down below. Now I understand that the Bride, through these words, wants to do great work for the service of God and the good of others; and thus she rejoices in losing her personal happiness and delight. Happiness and delight are flowers that belong more to life in the world than to life in the spirit. They seem to be lost, but actually the believer has all these elements when in this high state. Mary and Martha always go together: for in the active life (which seems to be outside), the inner side continues to operate. And when active works come from an inner source, they are admirable and perfumed flowers. They come from this tree of the love of God, and they are done for Him alone, without any thought of one's own interest. And the odor of these flowers spreads far and wide, to be of advantage to many.

Truly I believe that the individuals whom our Lord leads to this stage (that is, as far as I can understand), do not remember themselves anymore, as if they did not exist, as for thinking of their own gain or loss. They think only to serve and to fulfill the wishes of our Lord. Knowing the love that God has for His servants and His children, they are happy to be deprived of divine graces and comforts, in order to serve their neighbors, in order to tell them truths that are good for them and their spiritual progress, by the best way possible. They do not think about whether they themselves will be lost.

The progress of the others is always before their eyes. In order to fulfill the wishes of God, they forget about themselves for the good of their brothers and willingly lose their lives in trying to do this. In a few words, being drunk with celestial wine, and their words being wrapped in the sublime love of God, they do not care about themselves. And if the do remember themselves, they do not try to please men. These people make great progress.

Friar John of Saint Samson

It is good to communicate with such spirits, especially when they are touched, extended and drawn by enlightening and divine influences which from then on fill them without their noticing it. Because of the great facility and simplicity they develop, and because they talk very simply and very enlighteningly, their words reproduce simplicity in others who have the happiness to participate in these divine torrents of delights.

But those who are consumed, in whom all higher, deeper and simpler enlightenments have melted into one, these are always able to see everything, to reach everything, to judge everything, and to enlighten others by their abounding, simple, and very efficacious light. This light is given by intuition. This light, by its simple fecundity, simplifies and expands the inner selves which it has touched.

You know how hearts talk to each other, and how the farther people are from each other, the more their hearts communicate. This is even more true between us, because our affection is simple and unique in God, in whom we live. We talk together in a spirit of simplicity in spite of all that can be said of present and various events. What we prefer and what we like in each other is the life we share in the very same life of God, whose love pushes us always to love Him and to get lost in Him, to the last possible degree. Now we do see chaos in this century; however, we do not think about it, living current events, however they are, to divine providence.

9

SELF-EXAMINATION

A Short and Simple Way to Pray

Self-examination must be adapted to the stage the believer has reached. Those we are talking about must present themselves in front of God, who will enlighten them and let them know the nature of their sins. That kind of self-justification must be done in peace and quiet, expecting more from God than from their own search to reveal their sins.

When we search out our consciences with great effort, we can easily go wrong. It is easy to believe that good is bad and bad is good; and pride easily misleads us. But when we remain under the eyes of our God, His divine light shows us the smallest atoms. We must therefore leave our efforts, and abandon ourselves to God for His examination rather than self-examination.

As soon as we are in that state of prayer, God examines the soul, and He does not miss anything. All the believer has got to do is to turn himself simply toward God, suffering the pain and the punishment that comes from his sin being exposed by the light of God. At this stage of growth, as soon as a sin is committed, the believer will feel a sort of burning within, which brings its own reproach.

As this examination of the conscience by God is continuous, the person cannot examine himself any more. If he is true and abandons himself to God, the examination will be much better done by divine light than the individual could do it for himself, no matter how carefully he tries to examine himself. Believers who have chosen this way are often amazed by the fact that when they start to tell their sins, instead of the feeling of regret and act of contrition that they used to do, a sweet and peaceful love embraces their heart, as they sense God's forgiveness.

Those who do not know better want to get out of this stage. They want to make an act of contrition, because they have heard that it is necessary. They cannot see that they are losing sight of true contrition, which is this infinite love, infinitely bigger than what they could do by themselves. They should not try to do anything else while God is working in them and with them in the most excellent way. It is to hate sin as God hates it—indeed, to hate it in that way. God puts in the believer's heart the purest love. The believer must not therefore try to take any action. According to the advice of a wise man, "Put your trust in God; remain in peace wherever He has put you."

This believer will also be amazed at the fact that he will forget about his faults, and that he will have trouble remembering them; however, he must not worry, for two reasons. The first, because this forgetfulness is a sign that the sin has been forgiven and that it is better at this stage to forget everything that concerns us—to remember only God. The second reason is that God never fails, when one must confess, to show him his most serious sin. When He Himself makes the examination, the person will see that it is done in a much better way than if it were done by all the individual's own efforts.

This cannot be done at the earlier stages where the Christian is still in the active life. He can and must do everything more or less according to the stage he has reached. For those who are still at a lower stage, they must seek and follow good advice and they must not try to follow a way that is beyond them.

Have I spoken differently than
Catherine of Genoa

God's love touched Catherine's heart and gave her a very clear view of her misery and of the goodness of God, to such a point that she nearly fell on the ground. Seeing the sins she had committed against such a good God, she was cleansed of her sins, and she was purged of all worldly thoughts—so much so that she was shouting inside with very ardent love. No, she was not of this world anymore; no, she would not sin anymore; and if at the same moment a thousand worlds had existed, she would have given them up. She could not talk, not even open her mouth, because of her feeling of inner sweetness and the extreme love she was feeling. God, at the same moment that He gave her that sweet and loving wound, had pardoned all her sins, consuming them at the fire of His incredible love. However, wanting to do all things right, He made her pass through contrition. After that, she could not see anything but Him, so that she never saw again the slightest trace of her sins—as if they had been thrown to the bottom of the sea.

I saw some people crying for their misfortune and their bad propensities, and I saw the efforts they were making to resist them; but the more they fought to remedy their faults, the more they committed them. When someone was telling me all his miseries, I said to him, "You are unhappy and you are crying; I am unhappy also, and I do not cry. You sin and you cry for your sins; I commit sins also but I do not cry. You do wrong and deplore it; I would do likewise, if God Almighty did not stop me. You cannot help it and neither can I. Then it is necessary that we should stop thinking about ourselves, and that we should leave all things to the only One who can defend us against evil. And He will do what we cannot do ourselves. In this way you can be at peace with this bad part of yourself, which by its nature is always tormenting you. When it is thus imprisoned, bound by God, it is subjugated and does not talk to you anymore."

Catherine had no remorse, she could not find any sins in her and she was embarrassed and amazed that she did not know what to say. She tried to make a *general* confession because she felt that she must be hiding her sins. And although she felt alienated, she also found herself in a state of peace which she could not lose.

She continued, "I saw that God's light was so pure, that it could see such subtle things, could see so far, that I remained stunned by the great imperfections that it exposed in me, and I had to admit they existed. His love made me see many things which to me and to many others would have seemed just and perfect, but His love judged them wrong and imperfect. If I was talking about spiritual things—which I did often because the great fire which was consuming me often afflicted me and because the eye of God's love showed them and explained them to me—then straightaway Love overwhelmed me, telling me not to speak anymore.

"I did not know what to do or to say about such a subtle love which unburdened me so much. When this part of me found itself caught in its wrongdoing, I could not deny anymore the imperfections that love had discovered. I turned to Him and said: 'Since You have such a subtle eye and are so powerful, I surrender to You. Although the sensual part of me will be very hurt, please arrange everything according to Your pleasure and to Your will. Take from me this evil dress of pride, and clothe me with pure, clear, ardent and burning love. Oh pure Love by Your violence You make the slightest stain of imperfection into a hell, bigger and more rigorous than the hell of the damned!

This is what nobody will believe, will not be able to understand, apart from the one who has experienced it in You."

Friar John of Samson

Where real love is, there you will find a real feeling of pain for having offended God. I would call this feeling compunction rather than contrition. It is truly, I hope, impossible that such a believer, even though he has committed a sin, would be affected by great pain from this act. A truly loving believer examines and reviews his sins and shows the Doctor the little wounds of his heart. This saintly ignorance makes the believer simple: because at that moment he is all wrapped up in God. The Bride trusts her Beloved completely.

We will not talk here about contrition, as far as the true lovers of God are concerned, understanding that God's wish is only for love. Something that hurts God is when the believer has not returned His love—a love He has given, ardently, continuously, tirelessly. That pains Him, but it is a loving, sweet and kindly affliction.

The really spiritual person can see the least infringement and disturbance of his emotions or flesh. This seems to be the complete perfection of a really enlightened soul: to be able to recognize peace and disturbances. The more the believer is enlightened, the more he is calm, tranquil and peaceful within.

Monsignor Olier

I am not surprised about your depression and your ills. You pay too much attention to your sins, and they discourage you and perturb your peace.

Sin is a snake. It is so full of poison that it can kill just by looking at you. Unless you have always got antivenom with you, pay no attention to your sins. This antivenom is your divine Jesus. You could not look at the snake without running the danger of being fatally poisoned. This exposure weakens you from day to day, and you feel this by experience. If you continually look at your sins, you have nothing to raise your spirit and nothing to put you back on the right path. To contemplate your faults discourages you and lowers your spirits; and nothing sustains you.

Our Lord puts in the believer's heart, it seems to me, the hatred of his sins and enlightens him perfectly. He does that a thousand times better than the individual could do with all his discourses and imaginations.

Mr. du Bellai,, surprised by the fact that Francis of Sales did little preparation before he said Mass, said: "I am very surprised at the little preparation you do and the little thanks the you give before and after Mass. Even today, you were talking to a lady. You had been talking to her for about two hours. You bowed deeply to the altar, you got dressed, and you said Mass. After having said it, you took off your priestly habits and went back to your conversation." Francis of Sales replied to him, "My brother, I am amazed that you say so many prayers before and after Mass. But since I must answer your question, which only concerns my own disposition, I will tell you I would not know what other thing to do to prepare myself for such a great mystery. I can only think of bowing. I try to keep in the presence of God. I walk always under His eyes. Being continuously in the sight of God directs my soul completely. I try to see only God, and it seems to me that I desire Him only. It is God Himself who commands me to do what I do. I bend my mind to nothing; I am only an instrument in His hands to go where He wants me to go. I do His pleasure. I am always in the same mind, at the altar, in bed, and everywhere. Regarding my conversation with that lady I spoke to, I don't look at her personally; I only look at her in God, or rather I look at God in her. God wanted me to talk to her before and after Mass. I do all things in the same state of mind. This is all I am able to do, my brother."

Remember that the house of God is always in peace. Let yourself be led by His divine actions. Be simple in the favor He is granting you. Be active or passive or patient, according to the grace of God. Let yourself be carried. The Master has put you in rest; do not leave it until the Master tells you to do so.

Harphius said that the believer who has reached that stage must not care about sins of his past, and neither must he care about daily sins. He must not fear or worry about them, and he must abstain from self-examination and from searching for sins; for in such a search pride has a great place.

I have also written on self-examination in the book entitled

The Song of Songs

Delight in God is permanent and lasting when it is inside our deepest being. And because God is our final goal, we can continuously run to Him.

What essential union does is to strengthen the believer in such a way that he cannot have any more of these failings that new believers often have. Believers who still have a weak understanding of grace feel losses. But those who know union with God are confirmed in divine love, since at this time they are staying with God. Whoever is in God remains in love; for God is love.

Winter does not exist for a believer who has reached God. There is a mixture of the three other seasons which are united into one.

The Bride, having left herself and having surpassed all persons, meets her Beloved, who shows Himself to her with all sorts of attractive qualities. This convinces her that the happy moment of marriage is near and that a permanent union is going to bind them together.

A thousands shields are ready there to defend her against visible and invisible foes. She is armed by God with such force that she does not fear any assailant anymore, as long as she remains at such a stage—for here her stage is not yet permanent. Oh, Bride worthy of the angels' jealously, you have at last found your Beloved! You have got Him and you will not lose Him, ever.

The Beloved has found His Bride all abandoned, all melted, and all ready for the wedding, to be received by Him in a permanent stage. The Bride is perfect in herself because she has lost all interest in herself.

We must notice that whatever praises the Bridegroom has uttered to the Bride up to now, He has never said that she was unique and perfect. These qualities are only found in God, and when the believer is entirely lost in Him she enters into a permanent

56

and lasting stage.

Who is that person coming toward us, rising little by little, for we must know that the believer reaches God by rising little by little in this divine life. He rises up to God imperceptibly as the dawn, until the dawn becomes a perfect day and changes into noon, which is the glory of heaven. But the eternal day starts even in this life.

"Oh daughter of a Prince, oh daughter of God," cry the young girls, "how beautiful are you movements, whether inner or outer!" The inner steps are very beautiful, since she can always progress in God, while still resting. This is the beauty of this progress. It is real rest; and this rest does not hamper progress, neither does progress prevent rest. On the contrary, the more one rests, the more one progresses—the more peaceful is the rest. The outside steps are also beautiful, for the Bride is all ordained and led by the will of God and by the order of His providence. This great Artisan has wrought and melted His Bride in the furnace of His love.

She asks her Spouse to go everywhere with Him, for she has started to move freely and can still maintain her rest in Him. What she used to do not very well some little time ago, she now does perfectly. It is not she anymore, nor does she look at the fruit that is in her: but she sees that everything is in God. And yet she works with all her strength at any time God gives her work to do.

The first rest is a rest that has been promised. Then one gives a deposit and some kind of payment for the second kind of rest. The third is a continuous kind of rest, which will never be interrupted anymore, even though it is possible for it to be completely interrupted. The believer keeps her freedom, and it would be in vain that the Spouse would say "until she really wants to" if she could never want to arouse herself again. After a union of this nature, unless she is extremely unfaithful and ungrateful, the believer will never want to be separated from Him again. However, the divine Spouse in praising His spouse and acknowledging that she should be praised in His presence, wishes at the same time to instruct her more: to make her understand that only a vain complacency and contempt could introduce despicable ruination. So the third rest is the sleep in God, permanent and lasting. It is the peace of ecstasy, of sweet and continuous ecstasy, but an ecstasy that does not change the feelings. The believer has passed into her God by getting out of herself. It is a kind of peace which she will never leave.

In the next verse, God is going to put again before her eyes the lowness of her origin and how miserable her nature is, so that she may never cease being humble.

If the "highest waters" of afflictions, of contradictions, of miseries, of sins and setbacks have been unable to extinguish love, we must not believe "the streams of abandon" could cause love to be extinguished. It is they that preserve it. If man has enough courage to abandon all he possesses, even all of himself, in order to acquire this pure love, we cannot believe that he would later turn back to his old ways. This is not possible. God makes us know in this way the reality of this state and how difficult it is. A believer who finally reaches it will never come out of it.

It seems, oh my God, that you have taken pleasure in foreseeing the objections that one could have. One could say that this believer who has abandoned himself and does not act for himself anymore is not deserving anymore. You are, oh God, the God of peace, who has a vineyard that You let Your spouse mainly take care of; and the spouse *is* this very vineyard, situated in a place which is called "people": for You have made Your spouse fertile and mother of an innumerable people.

Certainly we are familiar with Saint Augustine's *Confessions*.

Saint Augustine

The childhood of the new man is spent nourishing himself from the milk of good examples that history puts before his eyes. From there he enters the second stage, which no more needs to be upheld by human authority. Forgetting everything that can be borrowed from men, he advances toward God. Enlightened by the lights of sovereign and immutable laws, he advances with a firm step toward the goal which God has set before him.

After this he goes on to another level where, strength increasing always, he comes to the point of practicing in a much firmer, much more sustained way what he had started to practice in the previous level. Now he acquires the level of maturity, of a full-grown man, capable of enduring unwaveringly all the storms of this world and all the attacks of persecution.

Then one comes to the fourth stage where man has risen above all that could cause him the slightest worry. He then enjoys in profound peace the abundance of treasures which are to be found in the peaceful and unchanging kingdom of sovereign and ineffable Wisdom.

This stage is followed by the fifth, which continues the renewal of the inner man up to his finest perfection. It also redraws in him the image and the resemblance of his God. The result of this is that one is in the world as if one was not there, and that one lives in advance the life that the redeemed will live in heaven.

The final stage is nothing but eternal rest and the kind of perfect happiness, always equal, unchanging, where there is no more distinction between stages. For as death is the end of the old man, eternal life is the end of the new. Death carries condemnation resulting from sin; and divine life is dressed in righteousness, and glory is its reward.

10

CONSISTENT LOVE

Henri Suso

This man is so closely in union with God that God himself becomes his foundation. The action of a man who has reached this stage is resignation. He does nothing else but to keep on doing nothing. He lives intimately with other men, but he is not impressed by things he sees. He likes them without being attached to them; and he sympathizes with their sorrows without himself worrying. He keeps his entire freedom.

Catherine of Genoa

The stage this believer has reached is a feeling of such great peace and tranquility that it seems to the believer that he is plunged with heart and entrails—inwardly and outwardly—in a deeply calmed and happy sea. He never leave this sea, whatever happens in this life. He remains motionless, and he cannot be disturbed. He is so unperturbed that it seems to him that he can feel nothing, either in his inner self or in his outer self, but a very sweet peace. This Love seems to say to the believer, put your accounts in order to make it so that whatever belongs to the world does not belong to you anymore. The more you progress, the more you will know why man has been created. You will know it is certainly to love, to enjoy, and to delight your Groom in this pure holy love. When man has reached, by the grace of God, this so-ardently-desired haven of pure love, he can do nothing more than love and rejoice, even if he was trying to do the contrary. And this grace that God gives to man is so admirable and surpasses so much any human desire or thought, that he feels even in this life he has been made to participate in the glory of the heavenlies.

I have, by the grace of God, an extreme happiness and a fearless kind of love. That is to say, this love never deserts me. Faith seems to me to be lost, and hope dead; because it seems that I am now keeping and owning what formerly I only believed in and hoped for.

This is a stage where the spirit stays with God in pure love without enthusiasm. This love is clear and simple, and makes the believer love God, even without finding reasons or thinking why he loves Him. This is the way God should be loved, that is to say, without fearing anything without hoping for a reward, and without considering how deserving of love God is, for this is the stage above reason.

Now the believer is one with God, who has taken possession of him and who works in him without his knowing anything about it, because he is being annihilated by divine intervention. From then on he stays in God always. He can say with the apostle: "Who will separate me from the love of God?" A continuous impression is made in the heart, that one lives always in God with this love. A heart loving God cannot be vanquished, because God is a formidable fortress in the sight of all enemies. A heart like this does not fear hell, nor does it expect joy in paradise. That is because this believer is so calm that for him, all that happens to him comes from the hand of God. He stays in peace through everything, and his heart remains motionless, being well established in God and fortified in his heart.

I feel so strong in spirit, and I have such great freedom that I have no fear that anything can take God from me. In Him I am happy.

61

Here is what Theresa has said concerning this topic.

Theresa

Such believers are rooted and have taken a firm stand in the truth. They do not look anywhere else for assurance and peace, but only where they know they can truly find it. They put themselves under the protection of our Lord, and they do not wish for anything else. It seems that the person enjoying the happiness we have described seems completely consumed and fortified by the Lord's shadow and by a divine cloud. From this cloud come sovereign influences; and a delicious dawn will scatter away the cares this world has given him.

John of the Cross

John of the Cross says that the believer lives on a mountain in a state of perpetual feast and that the "divine silence and the divine wisdom" are characteristic of this person. He says that only the honor and glory of God live on this mountain, and that the gifts and the fruit of the Holy Spirit are there. Now the believer wants and enjoys only the glory and honor of God, and is entirely transposed into God and made in His resemblance. This is because, through all of this, he is only searching for the honor and glory of God.

The believer will realize what ups and downs lie in this way and how, after the peace he has been enjoying, a tempest occurs and a lot of work is to be done. It seems this peace was given to prepare and encourage him to endure the present pain, being assured that after a storm, and after a time of misery, abundance and peace come. This is the way spiritual growth works, with its ups and downs, and the fact that it never stays at the same stage until one has reached peace. The stage of perfection, which means perfect love of God and contempt for oneself, cannot exist without these two parts, knowledge of God and of oneself. The believer must be experienced in one and the other. If he can humiliate the self while having appropriate appreciation of the self, he can develop perfect reflexes and then the highs and the lows will stop. Then he realizes union with God.

Consistent and perfect rest and quietness of this spiritual house has now been won by this believer (as much as the conditions of this life allow it) by actions of divine union which we have just enumerated.

The believer has received these secretly, away from the trouble the devil may cause, away from the flesh and emotions. In the secret places the believer has been quietened and strengthened, constant and stable to receive for a considerable time the experience of this union, which is the divine marriage between the believer and the Son of God. The devil fears believers who have attained such a state. When the believer gets to that stage virtues are so strengthened that there is no place where the devil can get in. This person enjoys the peace of God

This is the consummation of this stage, and a believer who is on this journey never rests until he gets here. This is because at this stage there is much more union with God and a more stable and assured peace than at the stage of the spiritual betrothal. It is about such a believer that Saint Paul has said, "I do not live for myself anymore, but

Jesus Christ lives in me." From then on, this believer leads a happy life, that is to say the life of God.

Nothing can happen to this believer anymore nor harm him, seeing that he has already walked away from himself and has entered the garden, where he enjoys peace and partakes of all sweetness.

The dove which came out of the ark came back with an olive branch, sign of the mercy of God who had made the waters recede. In the same way this believer has come out of the Ark of an all powerful God, who has created him. He has crossed the waters of sins, imperfections, sadness, and cares of this life, and then returns again to the Ark in the bosom of the Creator, with the olive branch. This is a sign of clemency and mercy which God has shown the believer in having raised him to such heights of perfection. Picture the earth of this believer, so to speak, being covered by the waters of sin. God stopped the waters and took them away. God has made the believer victorious from the attempts of his enemies who have always tried to prevent him from reaching his goal.

These believers have the same qualities, through participation in God, as God has by nature. They are like Him and they are God's companions. That is why Saint Peter has said: "Grace and peace be yours in the knowledge of God and of our Lord Jesus Christ. . . so that you may become companions of the divine nature."

Nicholas of Jesus-Maria

The passage from the Song of Songs: "You are all beautiful my Beloved, there is no stain in you." Gislerious explains it in this way. The Bride is completely beautiful, that is to say, in spirit, in soul, and in her flesh. Her flesh has been purged from other emotions and she is perfect in her virtue. Her soul is detached from any evil desire and adorned with wise precepts. Her spirit is free from even the tiniest influence of thoughts.

James of Jesus

Saint Thomas refers to a degree of perfect love. This love must be distinguished from the love which is still progressing, because in this world whatever perfect love one may have acquired, this love can still increase and progress. How is it possible that this love can increase, however advanced it is in this life, while at the same time there exists a degree of love which we call perfect? This degree of perfect love is distinct from the one which increases. Christians perfected in their spiritual growth still grow in love, but their main intention does not incline this way. Their main intention is to stay united to God. These are the virtues which come at the end, or the virtues of those who have already acquired a divine resemblance. Prudence only contemplates divine matters, temperance ignores earthly desires, strength ignores passions, justice is always allied to friendship with God and imitates it.

This perfection is so advanced that Saint Ambrose was able to say about Psalm 118, "They have already completely forgotten their sins, and this is rooted in them. And their progress is so great that they do not know sinful ways; and they would not be capable of committing a crime even if they wanted to."

John of Saint Samson

These believers have become unchangeable in the firmness of their intention, and very stable in their view and worship of God. God has done this for them and will always keep doing it more and more until they have gone to the farthest point, according to the order of His eternal foreknowledge.

Those who are most nearly perfect in this life are untouchable, impenetrable, immobile and unalterable in their inner parts, and there they live very far beyond their furthermost part.

It can be said of them that they are spirits; for they are so much clothed with and full of the qualities of the Spirit that their strength and their inner selves are singular, and nothing from outside can touch them or cause them concern. As far as their desires are concerned, they have completely transformed themselves by lovingly plunging into the infinite sea that He is. Beyond all this they have lost themselves in the essence of God without thinking of themselves nor of created things.

Now the one who has entered into the peace of God rests from his works, and God rested from His after the creation of all things. In this supreme unity nothing is seen nor heard nor separated that is distinguishable or separable. Here nothing is, except the eternal now. And here God only is, and He lives in the person who has become one with God by reflex of love. The believer has returned to his beginning in God before creation, yet he continues in his humanity, too. Even in glory, his humanity will remain, but will be completely penetrated by the non-created being, coalesced and completely lost in Him. He is still part of creation. In brief, we are not writing to be believed or heard (although maybe by a few) who have completely progressed to that stage. Theses spirits will have great pleasure to see themselves clearly as they are. Beyond that, in the eternal sea of eternal love which never ceases and which makes them lose everything, they will live their lives totally in His love—happily and gloriously.

By the same means, all that this fire has consumed and transformed, in faith and by faith, is itself without difference nor distinction; and this can be true in a believer. In fact, the believer thus consummated cannot rejoice intentionally or willingly. His strength is entirely consumed and he cannot have desires contrary to those of God. The life that lives on this plane is eternal, simple, and hyperessential, in peace and delight.

My Spouse, whatever I may say, I do not fear; for You are mine and I am Yours. You possess me, and I possess You. We are one.

So we may remain one in a unique way, simple in a simple way, without any alterations or variety. But our occupation, which is very important and for which we live, is to remain always true to ourselves, unalterable and immutable in whatever happens, as if we were steady rocks in an infinite sea where the waves beat outside without touching our foundation.

God is always Himself, and He cannot change. As for us, before we have been united to Him, we remain alienable and changeable in everything. We must try, according to our power, to remain stable and without changing in Him. This is the basis, the essence and the superiority of the purest and deepest spirits. This keeps all senses look-

64

ing inward in a very pure form of nakedness and everything is reduced to the supreme unity of the spirit. There remains no distinction between higher and lower. The spirit is simple and singular in the unity of God.

Now we turn to the author of
The Mystical Day

Taulere says that Albert the Great affirms that the center of a person's being, his spirit, is very marvelous, very pure and very certain—that it is the thing that cannot be taken away. It is his most inherent part, and that which perseveres the most; and no vexation and no adversity is found in it: no images, no sensuality, no mutability. It is without fancy. It cannot be hindered. The inmost center of the believer's being is fixed and unchanging because it never feels any vexation. And the pleasure that the spirit of the believer feels is free of any pain. Furthermore, it is not felt in his natural man. These are the words of Albert the Great, as recounted by Taulere.

11

CONVERSION

Conversion is abandoning the self to go back to God. Conversion is not perfect when it goes only from a state of sin to a state of grace. To be complete, it must change the outside and the inside. Once a person turns to God, it is then very easy for him to remain turned towards God. As time passes he will come nearer to God and become attached to Him. And the more he gets near to God, the more he goes away from the world. He becomes so strengthened in his conversion that walking this way becomes a habit. It becomes natural.

Now we must know that this does not happen by violent exercise of natural effort. The only exercise that a believer can and must do, being in a state of grace, is to make the effort to turn inside. After that, there is nothing else to do but to stay turned towards God in continual adhesion.

The person of God is attractive and makes the soul go towards Him. And attracting a person, God purifies him. The sun attracts to itself a course kind of steam, and little by little, without any other effort on the part of the steam but to let itself be drawn, the sun, bringing the steam nearer, refines and purifies it.

The Song of Songs

It is not possible to participate at the same time in two things very opposite to each other. It cannot happen, therefore, that one who has some participation with unity be divided and dissipated in two lives, if he keeps and continues with the participation he has with unity. That is why he must not be kept away from God nor enslaved by one of the affections by which unity can be divided. Those who approach baptism must get rid of all affections, even the least, which would keep them away from God. The new believer must put away from himself all communication he had with vice, which causes darkness in the soul. He must get rid of the bad habits and vicious affections that he used to have. Afterwards because he loves God he will be perfectly ready to be part of unity. He will be ready to aspire with all his might to this unity.

Now to the words of Saint Theresa concerning conversion.

Theresa

This happened, my Lord, since you kept me near you by your kindness, in order that I could not commit so many sins against you! When I withdrew from everything that you did not like, You started to show and to communicate Your treasures to Your servant. So it seems that You were waiting for nothing else but that I would have the will and the disposition to receive them. You very promptly started to give them to me and to want it known that You were giving me these graces.

12

CREATION

Here are my words found in my book on prayer*
A Short and Simple Way to Pray

Christians have been taught the end for which they are created, but they have not been taught to enjoy this end.

Sweet dependency on the Spirit of God is absolutely necessary; and it makes the believer reach, in a short time, the simplicity and unity for which he was created. When God redeems a person, He makes that person one with Himself, and singular, as He is. In order to reach the purpose for which we were created, we must abandon the multiplicity of our acts to enter into the simplicity and unity of God.

God, in creating us, created us in His image and likeness. He inspires in us the spirit of the Word of God through this breath of life He gave us when we were created in His image. With the breath of His life in us, we participate in the life the Word, which is in the image of His Father. Now this life is one—pure, simple, intimate and always fruitful.

The believer arrives at divine union only by putting his will to rest. He cannot live the life of God if he is not quiet in purity.

What one wishes for believers is this: that they take the shortest and easiest way; that they do not stop at the first stage; and that following the advice of Saint Paul, they let themselves be moved by the Spirit of grace which would lead them toward the end for which they have been created, which is to delight in God and to delight God.

It is a strange thing, we all know that we have been created only for this, yet it seems that we cannot let God lead us there in this life. We all know that the supreme

Catherine of Genoa

Take some food and eat it. After you have eaten it, its substance becomes nourishment and the rest is excremental. Nature gets rid of it as of something useless and harmful to the body. Imagine that this bread said to you: "Why do you take my being from me, since I do not like to be thus annihilated; if I could I would defend myself against you, which is natural to all creatures." You would answer it: "Bread, your being has been arranged to feed my body, which is worthier than you; and you must be happier with the aim you have been given in life than with your own being. Your being would not be worthy if it were not for the aim for which it was created. This aim gives you a dignity which you can only reach through being annihilated. Now if you only live to reach your aim you will not care about your being. You will say, 'Let me get quickly out of my being and put me on the road to the aim for which I have been created.'"

---

* The book formerly entitled *A Short and Simple Way to Pray* is now called *Experiencing the Depths of Jesus Christ* published by SeedSowers Publishing House.

When God has purified the spirit from the imperfections it caught through sin, the spirit is then drawn and goes towards the place for which it was created. The spirit, finding itself so beautiful, so clear, so worthy and so excellent, cannot find a place proper and suitable for itself except in God Himself who created it in His own image and likeness. The spirit of this believer is in such agreement with God and it has such an attachment for Him that if the believer could not stay with Him he would find any other place in the world to be like hell. The spirit, having been reduced and taken back to its proper being where it remains pure with God while being still alive, becomes such a subtle and small thing that man does not know it and does not hear it. It is like a drop of water thrown into the sea. If you look for it you can find nothing but the sea. The believer who has reached this stage is, even in this life, in a state of deep happiness.

John of the Cross

When saying "feeding at my mother's breast," the Bride means to say suckling, drying up and extinguishing the appetites and passions which are the breast and the milk of our mother Eve in our own flesh. These are hindrances if one wants to reach that elevated state. This being done, I find my spirit alone, that is to say, out of all things and out of myself in solitude and nakedness of the spirit. This happens, the appetites mentioned above having been suckled, that is to say dried up, and so alone I kiss You alone. That is to say my nature, already alone and without any temporal impurities, natural and spiritual, is united with You alone, with Your nature, by the only mean of love. This only happens in spiritual marriage, which is the kiss that the Bride gives to God. When the believer is at that stage, no one dares to attack him. In that state no devil, no flesh, no world, no appetites hinder it. Here is accomplished what is said in the Song of Songs: The winter is already gone, the rain has departed, the flowers have come.

Your mother, human nature, was raped in our first parents under the tree, but under the tree of the Cross, everything was made well for you.

So this sensitive part of the believer, with all its powers, strengths and weaknesses, at that stage is already subject to the spirit. And that is where a happy life comes. This happy life is like it was when you were in a state of innocence, where the whole harmony and capacity of the sensitive part of man helped him to be happier, and also helped him to know and love God better in peace and harmony with his more spiritual parts. Happy the Christian who reaches that stage!

This verse was put here to explain the tranquil and assured peace of the believer who has reached this very stage of progress. Fleshly desire is mostly seen among beginners and not among people having reached maturity. In these people passions have little or no power. The aim for which the Bride wanted to enter the cave of deepest love was to reach completely and perfectly, at least as much as this earthly life permits, what she had always tried to reach—that is to say, the entire and perfect love. Also to obtain perfectly, on the spiritual plane, the straightforwardness and clearness of the state of original justice. This verse shows two things: One of the things is that God shows the Bride what she was trying to reach in all her acts and intentions; that is to say, He shows her how to love her Spouse perfectly, as she loves herself. The second thing is that when she reaches there, God will also give her the purity and clearness that He had given in the state of original righteousness that was in her first parents. One could also say that God gave believers that state on the day of their redemption, perfecting, cleaning them up from their imperfections and darkness.

Nicholas of Jesus-Maria

About this passage of the Song, Saint Ambrose says: "I have taken off my robe, how will I put it on again? I have washed my feet, how will I get them dirty again?" The soul does not know how it will be able to put on again the clothes of the old man interwoven with the vices of sin. These clothes of the old man were left in the laundry of regeneration; for the study of penance and the forgetting of sins is already rooted in it. The strength of this regeneration is so strong that the believer goes back to spiritual childhood and there finds himself ignorant of the ways of sin, and is unable to admit crime, even if he wanted to, because he has lost all knowledge of sin.

Albert the Great: You will be without the ghosts of worldly and created things, and because of your willingness, you will be united in spirit with God—the more so as you get nearer to the state of innocence.

John of Saint Samson

We have then been created to be brought back to infinite Love actively, ardently, incomparably, purely and forever. This is achieved by the way of God's active and strongly efficacious love for us. It cannot be achieved any other way. All this is according to the order and results of His love for us. Of course, it requires that we love Him too. This we must pay for and send all our love lovingly, for we could never have done or given anything to Him which could reward and satisfy our infinite love. Compared to this love, man is nothing.

I have reached this point with you, My daughter and My wife: We are at the last stage of supreme satisfaction. I was avidly wanting to make you like Myself, until I made you die very sweetly between My arms in the infinite extent of My essence and My love. This is why I hold you so sweetly tight in the sweet and loving violence of My embrace, so that by this love which we both feel, you will become full of Me and enjoy Me completely along with all that I am. Therefore you are completely transformed above all transforming love, since you have reached your original essence which I am. You will live in Me and stay with Me. There will be no distinction, no difference between us, as much as that is possible. I am your rest and your complete happiness.

Angels cannot bear such a prodigious love as You, oh my God, have for poor fallen humanity. What contrast there is, oh eternal God, between what we had become and what we are now in You, our living Repairer. But this has been costly for You, and it has been accomplished by very supernatural and ineffable means.

We must go by a continual returning to our eternal and original sea; and nothing created must hinder us, however little it may be. This is why we were born. This is what makes us live. It is through this exercise that we get lost in all-consuming life, in which we want to plunge ourselves more and more without any thought of return.

13

DEFECTS
OR
FAULTS

A Short and Simple Way to Pray

As soon as we fall into some bad habits, we must turn inward. Because this defect has turned us away from God, we must, as soon as possible, turn back to Him.

It is very bad to worry about our faults; because worrying comes from secret pride and from love of our perfection. We find it very hard to look at what we really are.

If we lose courage we become even weaker; and the thoughts we have about our faults produce a pain which is worse than the fault. A really humble Christian is not astounded by his weaknesses; and the more he sees how miserable he is the more he abandons himself to God and tries to keep near Him, realizing how much he needs His support. We must behave this way because God Himself says to us: "I will tell you all that you must do, I will teach you which way you must take, and I will always keep an eye on you and lead you."

The Song of Songs

The most important graces of God always tend to a deeper knowledge of what we are. They would not be from Him if they did not give some experience of the misery of fallen man. The Bride has hardly left her Spouse's storeroom of riches, when she realizes that she is black.

What is black in you, incomparable lover? Let us know about it, we implore you. "I am black," she says, "because I see, in Your divine light so many faults that I had ignored up to now. I am black because I am not purified, but I am still beautiful—beautiful like the tents of cedar. I am beautiful because I am without stain. My Spouse makes me beautiful with His own beauty. The blacker I become in my eyes, the more beautiful I am in Him.

"I am black also through the crosses and persecutions which come to me from outside. But I am 'beautiful like the standards of Solomon,' since these crosses and this darkness make me like Him.

"I am black because there are weaknesses in my outer self, but I am beautiful because I am exempt from evil.

"I implore you, companions who have not yet reached a deep place in your inner selves, you who are only in the first steps of the spiritual life, do not judge me 'for the brown color' that I wear on the outside, nor for all my outer defects, whether real or apparent. My Lord, continually, ardently, and burningly looking at me, has 'discolored me,' as would a bright sun. He has removed my natural color to leave me only the color His ardor wants to give me. It is His love which dries my skin and makes it brown – not the fact that His love is leaving me."

This dark color is a progress, not a defect. It is a progress, however, that you must not think about—you who are advanced enough. It is a progress that is too delicate to be imitated. The dark color that you would try to give yourself would be a defect. It must come only from the Son of Righteousness, who for the good of the believer devours the bright color. His Bride's beauty of color had seemed so bright to her and to others that it had blinded her. It was a detriment to her. That is why He changed her color.

"My bothers, seeing me of this dark color, wanted to force me to take part again in active life. They wanted me to keep my appearance without trying to kill the passions of my inner soul. I long fought with them, but at last, incapable of resisting them, I did what they wanted. Trying to do outside, things that are alien to me, I did not keep my 'vine,' which is my very inner self where my God lives. And this is the only thing and the only vine that I must care for. And when I did not take care of my vine, when I did not make myself listen to my God, I became even less able to look after others."

The care one has of one's inner self makes one negligent of outer things. Because of this, the believer who is all enclosed in herself cannot take care of some small defects that Her Spouse will put right later.

The faithful lover prays the Spouse to remove the "little foxes," which are her defects. These defects damage the inner vine which is blooming in her innerself. And this is what makes the vine more pleasant and makes her love it more because she soon hopes to see the fruit of it. A young believer is so in love with herself that she could not survive it if He allowed the little foxes to destroy the flowers and fruit too early.

I turn your attention to
Catherine of Genoa

She lost all hope for herself, thinking man completely incurable. She did not want to waste anymore time trying to find some kind of remedy for the problem. Instead she put all her trust in God her love, and said to Him: "Lord, I give myself to You, because I cannot do otherwise. I am only able to make a hell of myself. That is why, Lord, I would like to do an exchange with You. I give into Your hands the bad part of me because You alone can hide it and engulf it in Your kindness; and You give me Your pure and clear love, which will extinguish in me any other love, make me completely abandoned to You, and make me so busy in You that nothing can remain of me." To which the very sweet Lord answered that He was happy with this. At that time the part that was troubling her was taken from her so that she did not remember it.

If the slightest sign of sin ever happens, the believer does not have any rest until he is clear of it and satisfied. The believer who lives in that loving peace cannot live in trouble—not with himself nor with others. If, with God's permission, it happens that a spirit used to divine love may be troubled, he finds it nearly unbearable because he is outside the peaceful paradise where he lives. And if God did not put him back where he usually lives, it would be nearly impossible for him to live at all.

Theresa

I will tell you something that happened to me when I was procurator. Some were often at their prayers because I had told them it was very good for them to be in prayer. Yet they could see that I had so few virtues, they were tempted and troubled by the fact that I was presuming to talk about prayer. And very rightly. They have told me since that they did not know what to say to others who were questioning. I was the reason why. Believing there was some good in me, they did not take into account that there could be some bad in me. And there certainly was. This makes community living difficult, however slight the sins may be. That must be why in several years only three persons gained some advantage from what I was telling them.

Now since I have been practicing prayer more, His Divine Majesty started to give me graces. God did not seem to desire anything; He only wanted me to be with Him. I often practiced a restful sort of prayer, and often received grace to be united with Him, and this grace sometimes lasted a long time.

I remained for some time in a state of worry and agitation of the spirit, ending in a long pain which I bore inside me with a lot of fear. I resolved to discuss all this with a spiritual counselor, so that he could tell me what kind of prayer I practiced and enlighten me on the way I was following, if by chance I had lost my way. I also resolved to do all that was possible not to offend God, for the weakness I saw in myself rendered me very shy.

Oh my God, how deceitful I was! I wanted to be good, but I went as far away as I could from good! The only remedy is being with the friends of God. It was very difficult for me to resolve to do this. I was wanting to wait until I would be better first, as when I finished my prayers. It is possible that I would never have gotten to that stage, because I was plunged very far in little sins, which were not enough to make me really bad, neither could they persuade me that I needed help and needed someone to give me a hand. Our Lord be blessed, for in the end, it was He who first came to my help.

John of the Cross

If everything God does is always for the believer's good, why is it that in this dark night of the soul God darkens the appetites and abilities, even when they concern good things? The believer cannot enjoy them or practice them in any way. I would answer that the emptiness of what the person does, and of his taste, even concerning spiritual matters, is a very reasonable thing for him to have. He has low and impure appetites and powers, and even if he were put in touch with divine, spiritual matters, he would not be in a state to receive them except on a very low plane. All that is spiritual is received within his spirit, according to his spiritual condition and whether he was prepared to receive it.

His natural abilities are neither pure nor strong, nor able to receive and taste spiritual things as they should be tasted in a divine manner. These natural powers can only taste the divine in their own natural ways. The believer's natural abilities must be weaned and reduced to nothing, so that the believer with all his abilities becomes able to receive, feel and taste what is divine. This cannot happen if firstly the old man does not die.

There are some people who have tastes, affections, and ability to use their powers toward God and spiritual things, who perhaps think that their communication with God is of the spirit. Actually their acts and appetites are only natural and human. These people have a temperament that permits them easily to move their natural powers in whatever way they feel. In order for the inner feelings and movement of the spirit to come to the point of being moved highly and divinely by God, the believer's natural powers must first be asleep, darkened and tranquilized until he swoons.

81

Therefore, oh spiritual one, when you find your appetites darkened, your affections dried, your powers inapt to any inner exercise, do not worry about that. On the contrary be happy about it, since God is delivering you from your own self, is taking away from you possibilities which you would not have known how to use so completely, so perfectly, nor with such certainty, because they were impure and heavy. Now God is taking you by the hand, and He leads you through the darkness as if you were blind. He leads you by ways you do not know and which you would never have found, however hale and hearty you are.

The reason why the believer walks without hesitation when he is in darkness is that usually, when he gets to a better stage and acquires more merits, he understands and thinks of nothing. Having never lived through this which dazzles the mind, the believer begins to think there is no hope for him. Rather than gaining merits and being on the right path, he feels that he has forgotten all that he knew, and he feels that God is leading him to a place where he has no feeling and cannot act. He is like a traveler who wants to go to alien and unknown lands which he has never experienced, but has only been told about. (It is obvious that he can only reach unknown lands by new and unknown ways, by leaving behind those he knew.) In the same way, the believer who is progressing walks in darkness and without knowing where he is going.

When the believer's spirit has become strong, the devil cannot do anything against that person. And not only that, this believer receives a new love with more assured peace. As he feels the seditions of the enemy, an admirable thing happens. The believer progresses further in his inner life because feeling that he is getting asylum, more hidden from the enemy, he enjoys peace, which the devil was unable to take from him. He goes on rejoicing because he possesses this tranquil peace and favor of the Lord. All this is hidden, and neither the world nor the devil can take it from him. He feels the truth of what the Spouse says in the Song of Songs. "See that the bed of Solomon is circled by sixty strong men because of night fears." The believer feels this peace and this strength, although he often feels his flesh and his bones being tortured.

Benoit of Canfield

At this stage, it is an imperfection to wish for God as if He were absent. In this wish is an act which hinders total abandonment to God.

It is being imperfect, as Saint Bonaventure says, to think of God through imaginary thoughts. One must not do it because it is an act contrary to total abandonment. One cannot do it because God is completely supernatural but thought is something natural. God is greater than we are, and above us, but our thought is smaller and below us. It is imperfect to look at God in any other way than simply remembering Him.

Finally, it is also imperfect even to take note of these sorts of imperfections, for if we observe them, we become preoccupied and active. Therefore, we must not look for these imperfections. If we do it we must do it very subtly, that is to say, as quickly as lightening, and then let it go.

Now we must not think that to have reached such a high stage of progress brings some diversity to this exercise. There are still many imperfections, but they can be corrected by one perfection. They exist and are remedied through one opposite thing, that is to say, nonexistence. Imperfections arise when man is something, thus perfection arises when he is nothing—when only God Himself lives and reigns.

Francis of Sales

Let us imagine Jesus at Pilate's place where soldiers, agents of His death, take off His clothes and then rip His skin with whips. After His resurrection He had a body that was immortal. He put on the clothes of a gardener.

Love did all this. And love enters a believer in order to make him die happily to himself and live again in God. The flesh must abandon its affection. For example its affection for pious exercises and perfection of virtues, which is the very life and comfort of any pious soul. When the believer has given up both his flesh and his piety, he has the right to cry: "I took off my clothes, why would I put them on again? I washed my feet from all sorts of affections, how could I get them dirty again? Naked I have come out of the hands of God, and naked I will go back to Him. The Lord has given me many desires, the Lord has taken them away. His Holy Name be blessed."

Yes, the same Lord who has made us desire virtues at our beginning, who makes us practice them always, This same Lord also takes away from us our love for virtues and for all spiritual exercises, so that more peacefully, more purely, and more simply, our affections would all be for the pleasure of his Divine Majesty. A beautiful and chaste lady named Judith used to keep in her closet her most beautiful dresses for special occasions. She did not like them, she never put them on. She never did, except when inspired by God. In the same way, since we have learned to practice virtues and devotional exercises, shouldn't we then love them? Or shouldn't we envelop our hearts with them? No, we must only do that when it pleases God—as Judith always wore her mourning clothes except on the occasion when God wanted her to be gloriously dressed. In the same way we should remain peacefully dressed in our miseries and abjection, in the middle of our imperfections and weaknesses, until God raises us to the practice of His actions.

One cannot remain for a long time in this nakedness, deprived of all sorts of affections. That is why, after we have taken off the clothes of the old Adam, we must put on the clothes of the new man Jesus Christ. For having renounced everything, even our affection for virtues (in order to want nothing except divine pleasure), after that we must put on again several affections, even the ones we had renounced and abandoned. But we must put them on again, not because they are pleasant, useful, honorable, or because they please our self-esteem. We must put them on again because they please God, they are useful to His honor, and they are for His glory.

John of Saint Samson

There is no need to talk about all this to a man who is good, who only has a good nature, and who remains and acts only through the feelings. He will never know anything better than good works, and will never renounce his ways, as he should when he finds himself incapable of doing them. That is why active life, which is more a life of feeling than anything else, seems very agreeable to these persons; and they endure willingly many sufferings because of the great merit they are expecting. They are full of their own ways, appetites and the things they are. They are totally ignorant of what they really are and of true good itself. They do not want to lose themselves, and if they sometimes lose themselves, they do not dare to lose the feeling and the taste for God. They abandon everything only little by little and in the least possible way, not wanting to believe that a life of renunciation, indifference to all things and resignation could be real holiness. This taste of God is a way to become used to holiness, and being used to holiness is the aim of life. And to get there we must live a life of renouncement. For what is such a life? It is a life made of holy practices that are practiced not so much in oneself as above oneself, being totally lost in God. It is His majesty that one always wants to satisfy, not wanting to please oneself.

It is strange that we can find men who have reached that stage but who can get out of it, to reason and speculate again, according to the strong activity of their senses, so that they come to be almost continually agitated by cares about everything. They shut their heart to God, prowling everywhere outside.

Some can see quite well in themselves and see that something is wrong, feeling themselves impure and disinclined to a life of introversion. Still they do not exchange these ordinary practices for exercises which would be more adapted to them, more useful for their good and their inner selves. They would probably need to be pushed hard and mercilessly, and have to pray to God very hard and ask Him to make them do such works and exercises. This is not what they want, and on the contrary, they fear this sort of thing like death. They will be forever untamed, captive and very strongly dominated by their own superiority.

Love among those who are spiritually mature knows how to be irritated patiently and to be humbly full of indignation. Men of mediocre virtue think we are in our own temperament because they are unfamiliar with our spiritual state. When we talk with them, we suppose *omnia licent* (everything is allowed). And often it is expedient for them to do the things which caused us to be irritated and indignant

14

DESIRE

A Short and Simple Way to Pray

God wishes to give Himself to us. Nothing is easier that to be in the presence of God and to enjoy Him. God is more in us than we are in ourselves. His wish to give Himself to us is stronger than the wish we have to possess Him. The Word possesses life, and since He naturally likes to communicate, He wishes to communicate life to men.

God, whose only wish is to communicate Himself to man, sends him many graces and a foretaste of His presence. Now God gives Himself according to the measure and aptitude He has put in an individual. But people are afraid to give themselves to God!

Catherine of Genoa

I feel that His divine goodness cares so much for the believer that there is not one person who, in order to win the world, even if he was sure of winning it, could have such a great love. Realizing how much love and care God must give us in order to lead us to His country, I am forced to say the our God seems to be our servant.

The Song of Songs

We must not believe that a believer who has reached the degree that the Bride has reached longs for the presence and for the sweet and continual enjoyment of the Spouse. Not at all. She used to desire ardently this sweet perfection, for this was necessary to make her progress and go towards Him. But now it is a hindrance. Her Beloved possesses her perfectly in His essence and in His power in a very real and continuous way, above time, place and manner. Now she does not need to sigh after moments of enjoyment, distinct and felt. She has given away everything to such a degree that she could not desire anything, not even the joys of heaven. This stage is the very sign that she is all possessed by God. That is why the Bride gives here this testimony to the Spouse, that she is happy for Him to go wherever He likes. Not because she despises His visits or divine comforts. No, she has too much respect and submission for the workings of God. It is because these kinds of graces are not needed any more to such an abandoned soul. In this state, having lost all her will completely to the will of God, she cannot desire anything anymore. The indifference of this lover is so great that she cannot lean on the side of enjoyment, nor on the side of deprivation. Death and life are all the same to her. Although her love is immensely stronger than it has ever been, she cannot even desire heaven, because she remains between the hands of her Spouse, as one who does not exist. This must be the result of the deepest annihilation. She is incapable to even wish to help others, and she can only do it under a special order of God.

Explanation

I intend to enumerate here some authorities who claim that one must not wish for anything. First, though, I am taking the liberty of relating an explanation that I gave to Archbishop Bosseut, who had taken the trouble to call on me. It seemed to me that this explanation was the only thing that he thought was not quite right, and I believe he will be convinced when he sees all the authorities that I am quoting here.

There are two kinds of delights. There is a mutable kind of desire, in other words bursts of desires which are distinct from each other. There is an immutable desire which is essential to man, that is, to return to his final end.

There is an excited kind of love which flames and ardors. Since this kind of love is distinct, it is always accompanied by felt desire. There is a quiet kind of love which ends in the death of self-will. The desire in this kind of love is restful, because of the peace and the death of self-will.

Love always comprises desire, but desire is like love. When a Christian is far from his God, love is impetuous, as well as desire. There is a kind of agitation which propels it towards its end. The nearer it gets to its end, the more its impetuosity diminishes. When love has united the lover and the Beloved, love and desire are peaceful. They are as if they were dead: This is a perfectly peaceful love, although it is the strongest kind of love.

There is a way to go to God through rising above oneself. This way is accompanied by ecstasies and ravishment. There is another way to get out of oneself by annihilation and nakedness. By this way there are no ecstasies, and it is a way that is completely like death. By this death the believer leaves the self behind and passes through a permanent state of ecstasy in God. Can we, already in this life, go to God and get annihilated in Him by a complete death of the will? None of those who have some experience of this stage can doubt it. It is what Saint John calls "to remain in Love."

"He who remains in Love remains in God." We must look again at Saint John's epistles. This is what Jesus Christ calls unity. Paul calls it transformation. John of the Cross calls it deification, as does John of Saint Samson. And these works use much stronger language than I do.

When a believer has flowed into his God because he has managed to lose himself completely in Him, he has lost everything he had. At that time he is like very pure gold. This does not mean that he cannot fall, because there is no such thing as sinlessness in this life. But God does not let it happen very often. What makes this believer pure is the fact that he has lost his will in the will of God. He cannot sin without taking his will away from the will of God, which is difficult. This does not prevent him from having certain outer defects which come from the fact that he cares very little about himself. But these defects are not evil, and God even uses these defects in order to keep this believer hidden from the admiration of others and hidden from himself.

It seems to me that it is easy to see that a person who puts his happiness in God alone cannot wish for his own happiness any more. No one can put all his happiness in God alone, except the person who lives in God in love. When the believer reaches that stage, he wishes for no other happiness than that of God Himself. Even the glory of heaven could not make this believer happy. If my love is in God alone, and for God alone, without thinking of myself, my desire is in God alone without any reference to myself.

This desire for God is not as strong as a lover's desire. This one desires only God and does not look for enjoyment in what he desires. He has the peace of a fulfilled and satisfied desire.

God is infinitely perfect, and the happiness of this believer is in the perfection of his God. Then desire is not like ordinary desire, which is waiting for what it desires. This is peaceful, as one who possesses what he desires. This prevents him from seeing all the good desires of those who love God in relation to themselves, nor does he understand the desires of those who love and search for themselves in the love that they have for God.

This does not prevent God from changing a person's disposition, at times making him feel the heaviness of his body which makes him say *Cupio dissolvi*, and *esse cum Christo*. At other times, feeling only love towards his brothers, without any relation to himself, he may wish to be cursed and separated from Jesus Christ for the love of his brothers. These dispositions which seem to be opposite can agree very well with each other if we consider them on the ground of faith which does not change. God gives happiness to the believer in Himself, for Himself, in whom the desires of the believer are at peace. Although the blessing of God is his essential happiness, God keeps awakening these desires when it pleases Him. These desires are not anymore like the desires of former times, which were in the individual will. These desires are stirred awake by God Himself. God is willing to do this because He now keeps the believer directly turned toward Him, and He makes the desires of this believer to exist without thinking. The believer cannot see the desires if God does not show them to him. Or it may be that his own words may make him aware of desires while he is sharing with others. Surely in order to desire for oneself, one must will for oneself. Now since all that God wants to do is to lose the will of the believer in His will, He also absorbs all other desires into the love of His divine will.

There is still another reason for which God takes away from and puts into the believer the desires of the senses, as He wishes. God, wanting to give something to this believer, makes him desire so as to be able to give him something. There is no doubt "that he grants the desire" of the heart and the "preparation of the heart." The Holy Spirit desires in the believer's heart and for him, and these desires are prayers and petitions of the Holy Spirit. Jesus Christ says to this believer, "I know that you always grant me what I wish." A violent desire for death, in such a one, would be certitude of death. To desire to be humiliated is far below wishing to enjoy God. However, when it pleased God to humiliate me through calumny, God gave me a strong hunger for humiliation. I call it hunger to distinguish it from desire. Some other times His hunger put in the believer the idea of praying for some particular things. At that time he feels that the prayer does not come from his own will but through the will of God. Such a person is not even free to pray for whomever he pleases, nor when he wishes. When he prays, his prayers are always answered. He knows it has nothing to do with him, but that it is the One who possesses him who grants His own requests through him.

(It seems that I can understand all this infinitely better than I can express it.)

It is the same thing for the gradient of the senses, or that which appears so, which is far less sentient. When a water is different from another which is flowing into it, there is rapid movement and some noise is noticed; but the gradient cannot be seen. The gradient, however, is still here; but it cannot be felt and is imperceptible, so that in a way it does not exist any more.

As long as the believer is not completely united to his God by a union which I call "permanent" to distinguish it from passing unions, he can feel his gradient towards God. The impulsiveness of this leaning is far from being perfect. Not-very-enlightened people think impulsiveness is a bad thing. This shows how far people are from God. When God has united Himself with the believer in such a way that He has received him into Himself, He keeps him "hidden with Jesus Christ." There the believer finds the kind of rest which excludes any leaning to the senses and which only by experiencing it can one understand it. It is not the kind of rest in peace in the sweetness of the felt presence of God. It is a peace *in* God Himself, a peace that flows into His greatness.

The light of the sun, if reflected by mirrors, would be brighter than the pure light of the air. However, these same mirrors which warm the brightness tarnish it and take away some of its purity. When the ray of the sun has something in it, it becomes full of atoms and it can be better distinguished than in the air. But then it does not have purity and simplicity.

The more things are simple and pure, the bigger they are. Nothing is simpler than water, nothing is purer; but this water, because of its fluidity has a great expanse. Because it has no qualities of its own, it can take on all sorts of impressions. Water has no taste, but it can take on any kind of taste. Water has no color of its own, but it can take on any color.

The spirit and the will, at that stage, are so pure and so simple that God gives them the color and the taste that He wishes—like water, which is sometimes red, sometimes blue, sometimes tinted by the color and taste given to it. It is certain that although one can give this water any color one wants because of its simplicity and purity, it is not true to say that the water itself has such taste and such color. By nature it is tasteless and colorless; and it is this tastelessness and lack of color which make it capable of taking on any taste or any color. This is what I feel in my spirit. My spirit has nothing that it can know in it or as belonging to it; and that is what gives it its purity. But it has all that is given to it, and exactly as it is given to it, without keeping anything to itself. If you asked this water what quality it has, it would answer that it has none. You would say, "but I saw you red." It would answer, "I believe you; however, I am not red: it is not my nature. I do not even think of all the tastes and all the colors that are given to me."

The same thing applies to the shape as well as to the color. As water is fluid and has no consistency, it can take the shape of any of the places it is put. It can take the shape of a round or square vase. If it had its own consistency, it could not take all these shapes, all these tastes, all these scents, and all these colors.

People can do only a few things while they keep their own consistency. The aim of God is to make them lose, by death to themselves, all attributes they have, so as to move them and to alter them as He pleases. Therefore, it is true that they have all kinds of shapes; and it is also true that the believers who have reached the stage we are talking about have no shape at all. This means that they feel only their simple nature, pure and without any impressions. When they talk or write about themselves, they deny they have any shape because they do not mention the changing situations where they are put. It does not matter to them. It only matters that they stay at the center of what they are, which is their continuing state.

Now we turn to other authorities.

Cassien

Prayer is perfect when all love, all desire, all application, all thought, all effort, all that we see, that we say, and that we hope for is God. Then the unity that exists between the Father and the Son has come to us. Then we obtain the result of the prayer of the Savior who said to His Father, "My Father, that they may be one, as I am one with You. I am in them and You are in Me, and I pray that they may be consumed in unity."

Rusbroche

The man who has abnegated his own will and who has given everything for everything, desiring nothing but the will of God, is the most free of all men. However, God, to test him and sanctify him, sometimes pushes him away from His right hand, puts him at His left hand, rushes him from heaven to hell, and having taken him away from all sweetness, allows that he be crushed by misery, so that he sees himself abandoned and held in scorn, not only by all men, but by God Himself.

Thomas A. Kempis

Some have burning desires which fly towards heaven and which , however, are not exempt from the temptation of human and carnal affections. Hence comes the fact that they asked, with such fire, for the goods of heaven. This action, however, is not quite pure and not for His sole glory. The desires that you have for heaven are often like theirs: mixed with worries. What is contaminated by love and self-interest is never pure nor really perfect.

Harphius

You must, as a general rule, realize that all we can ask of God or desire from Him, if it does not include a total abandonment of oneself for the love of God, is mixed with human nature and self-interest, even as far as things that seem holy and divine are concerned.

Catherine of Genoa

Catherine's purity and clearness of love was unutterable, and was bigger than human nature could imagine. And this love that God had given her was so abundant that she could not understand that it could grow more, because she was so full of it that she could not desire any more. What she had received kept her completely satisfied. This grace that God gives to man is so much bigger than any desire and any human thought that it makes those who receive it feel, even in this life, that they are made to share the glory of the heavenlies.

When God turns believers towards Him, regulates, orders and arranges their powers until He takes them out of their context so that the intelligence cannot understand anymore, memory cannot remember, nor the will desire, then such believers cannot think about what stage they have reached. Such a believer does not choose anymore, nor has he any more desire in heaven or on earth. With this kind of love he can love only those

91

God wants him to love. And God does not allow another person to know that pure and clear love in the same way as the first one feels it in his heart. It is different for each person.

In the year 1507, as she was praying, Catherine suddenly wanted to die. However, her will did not take part in this desire. It was only a natural desire of the spirit, soul and the body, in order to put an end to their torment. Because her love wanted to purify her completely, she wanted to extinguish all desires in her heart, in order to make His delightful residence. God made her remorseful because of that desire to die.

This desire had not come from her spirit. When she felt this remorse she used to say: "Love, I only want You: whichever way You wish. But at least if You do not want me to die yet, let me go and see others dying and being buried, so that I could see them when they are about to enjoy the great good that You do not want me to enjoy yet."

Her Love agreed to this: and thus, for sometime she went to see all those who died in the hospital and she also saw them buried. Then these desires and this will to see others die went completely away, her heart being united more tightly with her sweet Love.

One day a monk said to Catherine that she could die suddenly. Then the joy or the desire to die reawoke in her, and she said to him, "I feel a great joy awakening inside me. Oh, if such an hour could come!" Then these thoughts stopped forthwith.

From that day onward to the end, any kind of desire was extinguished in her, and she was still united and transformed by the will of her sweet Love. Thus she knew that any kind of desire indicates a lack of perfection; because the believer who still has some desires does not fully possess God, who is everything. The believer who is perfectly united to God finds everything in Him and cannot desire any other thing.

This intimate love, all pervading, sweet and gracious, which man feels in his heart, does not know itself nor does it know how to express itself nor can it understand itself except through man's spirit. In this love man feels fulfilled, bound, transformed, happy, peaceful and well-regulated as far as the senses of his body are concerned. There is no contradiction: this man has nothing, he lacks nothing, he desires nothing, and he remains at rest, peaceful and satisfied in his heart of hearts, knowing nothing else.

Memory is happy when it is occupied with spiritual things and cannot remember anything else; but it knows neither the way or the shape of it. The natural love in man, when it has been engulfed by supernatural Love, cannot care about anything else. It remains satisfied and happy, and it does not want nor look for any other kind of nourishment. It believes that it has all it could desire.

This state of mind gives great peace and happiness to such a believer. This satisfaction, however, does not lessen the torments. God could not make him suffer so much that he would wish to get out of this situation. The person does not get out of prison neither tries or desire to get out of it, until God does all that is necessary.

Theresa

This satisfaction touches the most intimate part of a Christian, but the person does not know from where it has come to him. Often he does not know what to do, what to desire, or what to ask for. It seems that he finds everything, and still he does not know what he has found. At that stage, man does not want to desire nor to have any other will than what our Lord gives him. Man gives God the keys to his own will.

Why should I care about myself, my Lord, and what care have I, apart from the care of You? There is neither honor, nor life, nor good of the body or the soul which could stop me, and I do not want nor desire any benefit for myself, but only Your glory. I do not believe that I should have been given so many good things so that I would lose my soul.

As for the Bride, it seems to her that there is nothing left for her to desire, but her very holy King has still a lot to give.

It astonishes me that the afflictions some have endured have caused them to want to die so that they could enjoy our Lord, and yet they afterward had such a will so serve Him and to praise Him, and to help some other person. All these feelings are so strong that not only they don't desire to die anymore, but they wish to live for many years.

John of the Cross

In this nakedness, the spirit finds rest because it desires nothing.

The believer does not have the desire of hope, either, because he is already happy and satisfied with the divine union. About the condition of present life, he has nothing to hope for, as far as the world is concerned, nor anything to desire for his spiritual life, since it is filled to overflowing with the wealth of God. He may still grow in love, and thus, whether he lives or dies, he wants to conform to the will of God.

Taulere

Pure love must not look for eternal happiness. That is to say, we must not want to enjoy a great glory in heaven, nor should we look for great honor and reward for our good deeds. These things and others like them are not to be looked for by perfect virtue and pure love. The love which is really pure leaves everything as if it did not care.

Other Comments

Saint Thomas: A believer's love reaches God Himself and should stop in Him. The believer does not expect that from there something will come back to him.

Saint Bernard: The Bride says, "I do not want Your blessing, but I want You Yourself. What is there in heaven for me? What do I want on earth but You!"

Rusbroche: God orders that we should love Him more than ourselves and above all things, without thinking of being rewarded. Love is the reward, and it is eternal life. Therefore, we must love without being loved in return and without forethought; for to love in order to be loved in return is a sign of dissolute love. It should be much more pleasant to believe, to hope, to trust in Him than to be assured of reaching eternal life. God commands us to love Him eternally, but He does not command us to want to be rewarded. Those who are good and just love the will of God more than their own, and would prefer to be in hell according to the will of God than to reign in heaven if such was not the will of God.

Bartholomew of the Martyrs: Those who live perfectly do not go towards God with a cheap and venal love, but with a filial love saying: "What is there for me in heaven; and apart from You what did I ever want on earth!"

Benedict of Canfield

Great surges of emotions, even though spiritual ones, are a hindrance, very different from a passive state which is sweet, deep, God-like, silent and immobile. This hindrance can be active and impetuous, restless and superficial. It can be too near to man, nature, and to natural and human actions. These two kinds of desires are like two kinds of water: one is bubbling and impetuous and makes a lot of noise; the other kind is sweet, silent, quiet, yet very deep. Although these bubbling desires seem good at first, they are not good at a higher stage and must be got rid of.

Good desires must not be abandoned, but their imperfection must be given up. We must not abandon them, but perfect them. We must not lose them, but purify them and perfect them in God. The seed is not lost, but is transformed and multiplies when a grain of wheat is thrown into the ground. In the same way desires are not lost because they are thrown into God, but they are purified, multiplied and achieve perfection. And as the grain does not become wheat if it does not die and rot, thus the good desires never lead to union and transformation, if they are not thrown into and consumed in God. That is why our Lord says, "If the grain of wheat does not fall into the earth and die, it remains alone; but if it dies, it bears much fruit."

As in the beginning the grain of wheat is needed, at the end its corruption is necessary in order that it can multiply. It is the same with good desires and their annihilation in order to acquire union with God. Of course, the grain is never really corrupted, but it is rather changed into wheat. These desires are never really annihilated, but rather changed and transformed into union. However, as the grain never returns to itself but remains transformed or changed into wheat, which is its purpose, thus desires must never come back, but remain transformed into union, which is their purpose. This is the only way they reach supreme perfection. The grain must not be thrown just anywhere and at any time, but in its proper place and at the proper time. In the same way, we must not abandon or annihilate those desires anywhere, but only in God, nor in any condition, but when progressing toward union with God. This must not be done at the beginning, but at the right time, which is after active life has been well-practiced.

This flowing of ardent desires into God is a change of practical love as far as enjoying God is concerned. This word flow contains two things, death and life. In other words, loss and gain. When the fervor flows out of the soul, it goes to sleep and dies, faints and is lost. But since it is lost in God, it becomes bigger and lives more than ever. That is why I do not use the word annihilation, as if they were annihilated in God, but I use the term a flow into God, for they are preserved in Him. That is why I do not say a deprivation of desires, but flow, to show that the desires were not present in order to be lost, but for the strong and sweet operation of God in the spirit of the believer.

Now this change contains three things: a clear manifestation of the thing wished for, a fulfillment of desires, and a disappearance of those desires. The first thing, that is the manifestation of the thing desired, which is God, does not come all at once, but little by little, as by degrees, according to the way our love grows. We must be careful to understand that in this state, it is an imperfection to desire God as if He were not there.

Francis of Sales

Assuredly our will can never die, nor can our own spirit; but sometimes it can pass beyond the limits of ordinary life, to live entirely in the divine will. At that point our will does not wish to will anymore, but abandons itself completely and without reservation to whatever pleases God. It is mixed and plunged so much into that good will of God that it disappears, and is all hidden with Jesus Christ in God, where the will continues to live no more as itself, but the will of God lives in it.

What happens to the light of the stars when the sun appears on our horizon? Certainly it does not perish; but it is swallowed and engulfed in the sovereign light of the sun, with which it is happily mixed and united. What happens to the human will when it is completely abandoned to divine wishes? It does not completely disappear, but it is so engulfed and mixed with the will of God that it cannot be seen anymore, and has no more will apart from the will of God.

Saint Francis continues, mentioning a voyage of Saint Louis and the queen. He concludes, "Madame, do not your want to go there as well?" "No, really I have no wish to go there, but I do wish to be near the king, and the places where he goes do not matter to me. I do not consider them apart from the fact that he will be there. I am going without desire to go. It is the king who goes and who wishes to go. As for myself I am not going anywhere. If I follow him I do not want to travel, but I only want the presence of the king."

A will which has left everything to God cannot have any wish but simply to follow God's wish. One who is in a boat does not move on his own, but lets himself be moved according to the movement of the vessel. In the same way, the heart which has decided to follow the will of God must have no other wish than to be carried along with the will of God. Then the heart does not say anymore, "Your will be done and not mine," for he has no more will to abandon. Instead, he says, "Lord, I leave my will in Your hands," as if he was no longer master of his own will, and trusted only in God. It is not really like servants who follow their master. Although the traveling is done because the master wishes it, they follow him by their own will, even as their own will is subject to that of their master. In the same way as the master and the servant are two different people, the will of the master and that of the servant are two different wills.

The will of one who has died to himself to live in the will of God has no particular wish remaining. The will is not only subject, but all annihilated in itself, and transformed into the will of God. One could say of a little child who has not yet the use of his will to be able to want or love something apart from the breast of his dear mother that he does not think of wanting anything else other than being between the arms of his mother. It is as if he is one and the same thing with her. He has no idea of agreeing with his mother, for he does not feel his own will and does not believe that he has one. He lets his mother decide what she thinks will be good for him. Assuredly this is the perfect state of our will when it is united to the will of our sovereign God.

We do not want to play as wishing things or wanting things, but we let God wish for and do things for us, as He will wish.

John of Saint Samson

In a perfect state of indifference we remain in a very pure, very peaceful, and very eternal love. We are there even beyond eternity, in the sense that we are totally lost even to the feelings and ideas which are even a little bit distinct from our Lord, who engulfs us and makes us feel lost more and more in Himself. Hence, we have no desire to get out of this place in order to reflect on our selves to see where we have gotten to and what we are.

Those who reside in the recesses of their innermost being are very marvelous here below. We must not talk to them about the circumference nor of what is not, but we can talk to them about penetration into the recesses of their spirits. And they will not be happy until they have penetrated this bottomless and bankless well, where God is alive to Himself and for Himself and where man is totally annihilated in God, so that he desires nothing else and could not bear to talk about anything else.

Surin Said:

The third stage is about those who have even given into the hands of God their salvation and their eternity. Nothing moves them because they serve God, and because they love Him with a pure love.

The way of the good and the spiritual is not to have any desires for anything, but to be indifferent to everything, and to look only for the will of God because they love Him with a pure love. Although they may not feel any actual love, they continue in this way through sheer faith. Looking for the divine will, you must first of all look for union with God by conformity with the will of God. Then you must try and experience God through this fulfilling union where happiness is found.

Louis, Abbott of Estival
tells us

Quoting Sister Marie Rosette: I feel and I know, even without thinking about it, what I want to do for God, for His pure love, for His greater glory, with all purity, having abandoned all I could do for myself. However, I never really think about it, nor think about wanting God. I think that as I am leaving Him everything to do with my will and I am asking Him to choose everything in my place, keeping no will or choice in time or in eternity, I must leave it to Him to will for me. Therefore, I want nothing of the things of this earth nor of heaven. Whatever God wishes for me is enough for me. If I could enjoy God eternally, even if there were no sweetness or satisfaction in it, which is impossible, I would still be happy.

My attraction and my instinct, if I have one, would rather move me to see nothing, to do nothing, even not to decide if I can or if I should do something, but rather to walk blindly on and to lose myself in God, so much so that I cannot even see that I am losing myself. And as I am losing myself, or as God even makes me get lost, my spiritual powers are so tied up that I can at no time use them to perform inner spiritual exercises. I am never more peaceful spiritually, and I never feel better in my inner self, than when I let myself be at the mercy of this desire to do nothing.

When something is lost, the person who lost it does not see it anymore, nor does he use it. In the same way when a believer has completely abandoned himself to God, plunging into Him completely, he is lost in God along with all his spiritual powers, and he could not use them unless he came out of God to find himself again. He loses himself in God in order not to be himself anymore and not to live for himself, but to be entirely given to God, so that God can live in him. Therefore, God must live in him, act for him and will do anything He wishes.

My spiritual powers are like instruments which I use to reach union with my God. I do not need these spiritual powers to arrive at this union, since it is already done. My soul has been united with God for several years. I never think that I should say to Him words of love nor of trust, nor of abandonment. I do not feel that I should have these feelings, and should not desire to have them. If God gives them to me, I receive them; if not, I do not try to ask Him for anything, either for me or for others. When I am in a state of dryness I do not try to submit to Him or to dispose myself to suffer, nor do I try to do anything whatever. Finally, it seems to me impossible to do anything nor to wish for anything, but that the will of God be done eternally in me and all creatures. I do not try to desire this, but this is my inner position. I feel no resistance as far as my will is concerned in accepting and enduring everything God could wish, even if it were the punishment of hell for eternity.

What we must do is to do nothing—and not even want to do nothing. My wish is to wish for nothing, my will is not to will anything, my inclination is not to have any, my choice is not to make any choice. I do not even wish to desire not to desire anything because I think that this would be some kind of desire. I do not want to think nor wonder if I desire not to have any desire, in order to engulf myself completely and to go forward without any support other than God Himself.

I try not to be distracted. I wish for neither honors nor contempt, joy nor sadness, sweetness nor dryness, satisfaction nor desolation, health nor illness, death nor life, heaven nor hell, nor any of the things that one may desire in this world or in the other world. All that attracts me and all my inner instinct, if I have any or if I show any, rather incline me to see nothing of all of this and to do nothing at all.

15

THE ROLE OF
THE MIND

The Song of Songs

The believer can only know the Lord's love if he has an understanding of himself. The next necessity is for the Christian to realize that he is nothing. This helps him move toward the completeness of God. Seeing the all of God, we get glimpses of the abyss of our nothingness.

What the believer must do is let go of what little he believes he understands of God. He must see God only through the eyes of love, not in a theological way. His eyes must be veiled—as the seraphim. The eyes of the believer look upon his Lord with no thoughts of this life at all. This does not mean he will have no understanding, as God Himself is free to bring forth discoveries in the heart of the one who has fastened his eyes on the Lord only. The Word speaks to him all the time. To be taught from God in such a state is ineffable. The believer is kept in the Lord's presence, and love flows back and forth between the believer and his Lord.

Thomas A. Kempis

Happy is the one whom God teaches, not through images and words but by means of God Himself.

The more a believer quiets his inward self, the more he stays deep within his heart, the easier it will be for him to go forward in the understanding of the Lord. Furthermore, the more he will be able to understand the purpose of the difficulties in life. This is because he will receive a gift that is not part of intelligence or human knowledge, but is from God Himself.

There is a great difference between the vision man has and the enlightenment of a man whom God Himself teaches through His own Spirit. The science of a very clever theologian is far distant from that which God speaks within the heart of a simple believer in ways that have nothing to do with words. The enlightenment which comes from God—by His grace—is a noble thing and far more excellent than human knowledge which is acquired through man's effort.

John of the Cross

If a believer looks back upon his earlier life and realizes that what he and everyone else knew was pure ignorance, he will be able to compare it with that which has been imparted by the Savior. Nor does the believer have any interest in going back to the former way of obtaining what he once thought was "revelation."

If there is a highest wisdom of God, then that is what the Lord is inviting the Bride to have. In this pictorial book, God's wisdom is represented by a high mountain. The Bride says, "Let us go to the mountain that I might understand your beauty." The Bride is saying, "Make me become like You. Let me know something about Your beauty, about Your divine ways. Let me know the Son of God." In that place of love the believer comes to understand the purpose of God's work in creation.

What God imparts to the believer does not come in the noise of words, nor are the senses particularly involved. It is more like the silence and peace of the night. What

God reveals to the believer has nothing at all to do with the senses or the emotions. Call it understanding without understanding! Human understanding operates in the midst of lies and shadows. But God teaches the believer in those moments that have nothing to do with words. His enlightenment is found in quietness. There is no noise there, no phantoms, no shadows.

Now let us look at the words of

John of Saint Samson

"Oh my love, devoted ignorance is not a bad thing for the believer." We are loving with love that is above love. (I detest trying to explain this or even to consider it on a more human level.) We do not desire the knowledge of intimate love. The less you desire and think about these things the more likely you are to possess them.

You are my life. Just the word love spoken by You, that is enough for me.

In the moment of being touched by God's love, we cannot explain anything though we are steeped at that very moment in love. And yet the word love is only a word. And the love we have in our hearts is what He produces in us, and it is of Himself.

There is nothing to compare to You, my Lord!

The man who has been ravished by God has for a moment known oneness with Him. He has touched something of the eternal future and its blessed state. No longer will his delight be found in nature and in physical creation.

Now we turn to

The Mystical Day

The author of *The Mystical Day* says prayer is an elevation of the soul in God, and it is reciprocal communication between the believer and his Creator. The Lord shares His secrets and revelations to the believer and reveals His mystery to him. The Lord does this in order to be loved by the believer. How does the believer come to love God? By God making Himself known to the believer. Nonetheless, God gives this grace only to one who is very small in his own eyes and who remains in this low state as he stands in the presence of God. The believer does this because he knows he is nothing. He admits his weakness and his unworthiness.

A Short and Simple Way to Pray

It is impossible to separate the two verbs, to speak and to understand. The reason why inner silence is so necessary is that you must listen carefully and pay attention in order to hear and receive the eternal Word.

Hearing is the sense which is made to receive words communicated to it. Hearing is a more passive than active sense; it receive and does not communicate. The Word being what must be communicated to the believer, he must be attentive to the Word who wants to speak to his inner self. That is why there are so many passages which urge us to listen to God, and render us attentive to His voice.

Listen to Me all of you who are My people: nation that I have chosen.

Listen to Me all of you whom I carry in My breast, and who are the sons of My heart.

Listen, My daughter, see and be attentive: forget the house of your father, and the King will love your beauty.

We must listen to God, be attentive to Him, forget ourselves and all that interests us. Only these two acts (or rather passions, for it is a very passive thing) attract His love for the beauty which He Himself has given us.

Outside silence is very necessary while learning to cultivate inner silence. It is impossible to strengthen inner life if one does not love silence and retreat. God tells us this through His prophets. He leads believers into solitude and there He talks to their hearts. The way to care for God in the inner self cannot exist when you try to be busy outside with all the nonsense that presents itself to your mind.

Oh if only you knew how happy you can be when you listen to God in this way, and how you are strengthened by it! "All flesh must be silent in the presence of the Lord."

The Song of Songs

The Bride, who is asleep for everything else, is most attentive to the voice of her Beloved. She first hears the voice. "Here is the voice of my Beloved," she says. "I know it, I hear it, and the effect it has on me makes me know that it is the voice of my Beloved." I have said in many places that His voice is difficult to be heard. All this is comprised in the word *hearing*.

Thomas A. Kempis

The one who listens to the eternal Word does not bother about useless questions. Everything has been done through the Word, this sovereign voice who speaks to our hearts. Without the Word nobody can really understand things nor judge them sanely. The one who finds everything in the sovereign unity, the one who relates everything to this unity and who sees everything though this unity, will keep his heart at peace in God. God, make me one with You, attaching me to You by eternal love! I am often bored with so much reading and so much listening: I find in You alone all that I am looking for. Let all the wise men be silent in Your presence; You only can talk to me.

I will listen to what the Lord says to my heart. Happy is the Christian who listens to God, who talks to Him, and who receives from His mouth words of comfort! Happy is the ear that hears the sacred sound of this divine language and makes itself deaf to the noise and turmoil of the world! I repeat once again, happy is the ear which does not listen to words from outside, but hears the very truth.

Speak, Lord, because Your servant is listening! I am Your servant; give me understanding of what You are ordering me to do. Make my heart obedient to the words that come from Your mouth, and make them penetrate my soul as celestial dew.

Once the Israelites said to Moses: "Talk to us and we will listen: but may the Lord not talk, as we are afraid we may die."

It is not the kind of prayer that my human nature would pray, my Lord. No, I do not pray You to do this, but I do ask You humbly to give me the grace that the prophet Samuel asked for: "Speak, Lord, because Your servant is listening."

I do not wish Moses nor any of the prophets to speak to me, unless You talk to me Yourself, my Lord and my God, You who have been the light to all the prophets. For by Yourself, without them, You can teach me everything; and they without You would be no use to me. The prophets can make their words be heard, but they cannot grant graces and spirit. What they say is wonderful, but the heart is not moved if You Yourself do not speak to it. Talk to me because Your servant is listening and because Your words have the power to grant eternal life.

My son, listen to My words full of heavenly sweetness which infinitely excels the presumptuous science of all the wise men in the world. My words are spirit and life, and they must not be considered by human thought. You must not listen to them to find in them a vain love, but you must receive them in silence, in deep humility and great affections. I am the Sovereign Truth. I will teach you what is right and what pleases Me. I am the one who teaches without the noise of words.

Catherine of Genoa

The spirit can understand more than the tongue can express, but the tongue cannot remain silent. It cannot say what it would wish to say because if the mind has not been enlightened by grace, it only understands these things vaguely.

John of the Cross

God cannot be clearly understood simply by intellect. The Lord said, "If there are any prophets among you I will teach them through visions, or I will talk to them in dreams. But there is no one like My servant Moses, who in My house is most faithful: for I talk to him intimately."

The reason why it was proper that priests and prophets under the old law could ask God for visions and revelations was that at that time faith was not yet on a very secure basis, nor was the evangelical law established. People then needed God to talk to them, sometimes by words, sometimes by visions or revelations, and at other times by signs. What God answered and revealed were mysteries of our faith. But now that our faith is based on Jesus Christ, and the law of the gospel is evident through the state of grace, we must not worry about signs and visions anymore, nor want God to answer as He did before. Giving us His Son who is His Word and His Promise, God has told us and revealed to us all things, once and for all.

About theses substantial words, the believer does not have to do anything or wish for anything, but must keep these words with resignation and humility, saying freely yes to God. You have nothing to fear. You must not work to hope for what you desire, because with these substantial words God acts in you and with you. You do not have to reject anything because the grace of God remains in you, full of the gifts of God. Your inner feelings are very high, very eminent, and very useful, and the believer cannot know where they come from, nor does he know which good works God rewards him for. God's favors do not depend on good works. God gives His graces to whom He pleases and for whatever reason pleases Him.

The essence of this kind of silent prayer is the language God uses with our spirit. Our physical senses cannot understand this language of the spirit, nor can they express it.

It is as if the believer were saying: I feel something that I know remains hidden. It is a sublime trace of God uncovered for the believer that must be followed, a very high knowledge of God which cannot be explained. This is why we call it "I don't know what." This sometimes happens to believers who have reached a very high stage in what they see or hear or know. God gives them a forewarning. He lets them feel the greatness of God. The believer thinks so highly of God that he understands clearly that he has everything about God which is to be understood. And this feeling, which cannot be properly understood, is a very excellent, elevated and very eminent stage of knowledge.

One of the greatest favors that God can give is when He comes into our lives and makes us clearly understand that it is impossible to understand Him thoroughly. We are not in the position of those who see Him in heaven. A believer's experience of God will not make him able to understand God. Since his experience is not really understood, it cannot be expressed, although it can be felt.

All these actions are designed because the believer is moved by God. This flame burns brightly, making the believer love God. This is the language that God speaks and which He uses with those who have been purified. These are words that are all aglow. "Your words are blazing," said David. These words "are spirit and life." People who are able to hear these special words feel the virtue of the words. But those who cannot taste such things cannot appreciate the spirit of the life which is in them.

This is why the Son of God was not appreciated, because the hearers were impure. Such people do not appreciate the language of God, even when He talks to the inner man. Saint Peter did appreciate His words when he replied to Jesus Christ: "Lord, to whom would we go? You have the words of eternal life." And the Samaritan woman forgot about the water and her pot when she heard the words of God.

When the believer is very near His Divine Majesty, he is engulfed in flames of love. In those flames of the Holy Spirit, the believer may have a taste of eternal life, although that taste is not perfect. The conditions of this life here on earth do not allow it to be perfect. That is why the believer calls this flame bright. This flame is always bright, but at this particular stage the believer feels that the taste of the life of God is so alive that the spirit and the senses can vividly appreciate God. That causes the believer to rejoice in the living God. As a result, the believer feels God vividly in this flame. He cries out: "Oh bright flame, Oh holy ardor!"

I now quote
Nicholas of Jesus-Maria
as he tells us what others have said.

Nicholas quotes many Roman Catholics who have been sainted by the Catholic church. Here are quotes he has given us of Christians who have come before us.

Saint Thomas: God created all things by His word.

Saint Bernard: The tongue of the Word shows the favor of His kindness; but the tongue of the soul is the fervor of his devotion. When the Word moves His tongue, wishing to speak to the believer, the believer would not know how *not* to feel it. The Word says to the believer, "You are beautiful." This gives the believer the ability to love. And to make the believer know he is loved, the Word says to the believer, "You are My friend." Hence, when the Word speaks, it is to give God's grace, and the response of the believer is admiration and giving thanks.

Saint Theresa: When I was in great anguish, these words were enough to get me out of my anguish: "Do not fear, My daughter, I will not abandon you."

It seemed to me, according to that state I was in, I would need several hours to convince myself to be at peace. I thought nobody could convince me. There I was, in peace and quiet with strength, courage, confidence, and light. In one instant my soul was completely changed. I was sure this was done by the Spirit of God. Oh, marvelous love of God, His words are truly words of love. And thus I said: Who is He who makes all my spiritual powers obey! In one moment He gives light in such darkness!

Saint Bonaventure: Consider that the word of God which comes out His mouth does not return to God empty. The word of God is fruitful; it does everything for which it has been sent. So you can say, "The grace of God has not been empty for me."

Thomas of Villeneuve: I believe this happens to the saints in this life when God speaks to them, not through the Scriptures, but when He Himself speaks. When the Spirit speaks, everything else is disgusting!

Saint Gregory (Also speaking of the intuitive word of God): In order to answer God, the voluntary expectation of His visit must be poured into the spirit of the believer.

Bartholomew of the Martyrs has well demonstrated that these words happen when the spirit of the believer is silent. When the faculties of the spirit are silent and stop any actions of their own, God Himself speaks as He wishes. He creates in the believer a very noble and very marvelous work. Samuel wanted to express this when he said to God: "Speak Lord, because your servant is listening."

Saint Bernard: "I admit that the Word has come to me several times, but although the Word often came, I did not feel anything. Sometimes when He came I felt His presence, I remembered that He was present. I have been able to feel that He was going to come, but never have I really felt Him. Where did He come from when He came into my spirit? Where did He go when He left my spirit? How did He manage to get in or out? I prefer not knowing.

"You do not know where God is going or where He comes from"; however, there is nothing extraordinary about this. The Word, as Groom, sometimes comes into my soul in this way. He has never given me notice that He was coming, neither by talking, nor by a feeling of beauty.

Saint Bonaventure: Sometimes, oh sweet Jesus, when I am searching for You and when my eyes are closed, You put in the mouth of my heart what we are not allowed to know.

James of Jesus

tells us:

Saint Bernard: It is possible that I may be asked what it is to enjoy the presence of the Word. I would answer that the Word rather looks for someone who has already experienced Him. As for myself, if I ever enjoyed His presence, do you think I would be able to express what is ineffable? Listen to a man who has had this experience: "If my spirit is in excess beside God, it is for God; if my spirit is moderate, it is for you." That is to say: It is another matter with God, He is the only arbiter. It is not the same with you.

I have been allowed to experience this situation, but not to explain it.

Oh you who want to know what it is to enjoy the Word, prepare not your ear, but your spirit! You will not know anything through words, but grace will teach you everything. God is hidden from wise men and those who are prudent, but He reveals Himself to the little ones. Brethren, humility is a great and sublime virtue which deserves what is not taught to her. Simplicity is worthy of conceiving what could not be taught to it: worthy of conceiving through the Word and from the Word what it cannot express in words! Why is this? It is not that the Christian deserves it; but because such is the will of the Word, the Bridegroom, our Lord Jesus Christ.

In such elevated and spiritual persons, where experience is greater than doctrine, where those who know cannot express it, where the tongue is not the mistress, where humility learns what it cannot teach—in this situation the substantial Word of the Father produces such marvels as are impossible to be expressed. Then we must not try to rule our lives through the intellect nor by rules given by masters. In communication with God as Bridegroom, in experience and heavenly sweetness—herein is the school where we are taught. Here clarity is harmful, darkness enlightens. Here we must only look at what we see. This is not acquired through speeches but through the fire of love. Here the death of holy despair is a true disposition for this divine life. How can we put order into these matters and find the ways through which to explain such high things? Wishing to express what is immense and inexpressible, we should go through ordinary rules, without exceeding common vocabulary which is used in ordinary language.

Francis of Sales

Sometimes not only does the believer notice the presence of God, but hears Him speak through some inner enlightenment and communication which serve as words.

Sometimes he feels Him speak and talks to Him as well. But this happens so secretly and in such a low voice that the holy peace and quiet is preserved; and the believer's spirit, without his awakening, keeps vigil with God. That is to say, the spirit keeps vigil and talks as a heart to her Beloved, with as much sweetness and rest as if it were sweetly asleep. And some other time the Bride feels the Bridegroom talking to her; but she cannot talk to Him, because the pleasure she has in hearing Him or the reverence she has for Him keeps her silent. Or it may be that she is going through a period of dryness and is depressed, so that she can only hear Him and is not able to talk to Him. This happens in the physical body to those who are beginning to go to sleep or are much weakened by some illness. But sometimes the Bride neither hears her Beloved nor talks to Him. Neither can she feel any sign of His presence.

John of Saint Samson

What I have just told you, oh My daughter and My Bride, this is why I want to show you your own being. I have to tell you everything and make sure you understand everything, for what I work in your spirit is what I say to you. It is our loving conversation, not only in all these things, but infinitely more. In this consists our common enjoyment and our common peace.

This, My Daughter My Bride, is what I operate in you and what you are in Me. My humanity and My divinity both still exist, one different from the other, one in the other, and one for the other. In the same way, proportionately and in some way, your humanity which has not become divine continues. I possess fully, for Myself, all the happiness that comes from My nature, and it flows to you through My love, the simple and ample flow of My happiness, proportionately to what you are and of what you possess in Me. All this will make you fulfilled.

I hope you understand Me well: All these secrets are yours. As for Me, I keep the deeper, more amorous and more intimate excesses of our love a secret. I repeat, we possess each other through an equal and reciprocal love, and our happiness is the same. Thus, wherever you go, you will never be without Me and without My glory; and going out without going out you will come back in Me and enjoy Me and My glory, as if you had never gone out.

16

DEALING WITH DISTRACTION

Distractions should be listed along with temptations since both will be dealt with in the same way.

Here is what I have said about distractions in the book

*A Short and Simple Way to Pray**

The main aim of the Christian is the presence of God. Those who try to oppose their senses increase them. Instead, by delving into the faith of the presence of God and by recollecting one's senses, one can deal with distractions.

You stand against distractions indirectly, not directly. Be as a little child when he is distracted by something that might cause him to fear. He simply hides in the bosom of his mother.

"God is in the center of your spirit and he will not be shaken."

It is not to fight your enemy, it is not to fight temptation nor distraction. If you do that, you will be left wounded. Vanquished. Instead, quietly return to the presence of God, and them you will find yourself strengthened.

Listen to the words of David: "The Lord is always in front of me, and I will not be moved; this is why my heart is joyful and my flesh can rest in safety."

Once more let us return to

Thomas A. Kempis

You will overcome distractions by doing so little by little, by doing so with patience through waiting. Wait before God with humility. This is far better than trying to avoid distractions.

I will have no fear of falling. I accept the distraction. I will wait with humble patience. I wait for the storm to pass and for peace to return. You are powerful enough to lead me out of temptation. This is a grace which You have already given to me, oh my forgiving God!

What did Theresa have to say about temptations

Theresa

Do not care about the fact that your mind wanders. Sometimes I think the Lord wants to give us distractions perhaps to discover who they are who love Him enough to help Him carry His cross—the cross given to each person. He may want to see them pass

---

* The book formerly entitled *A Short and Simple Way to Pray* is now called *Experiencing the Depths of Jesus Christ* published by SeedSowers Publishing House.

through such tests before He gives them His great treasures.

Those who know Him well do not ask to be delivered from temptations and distractions, which are proof that it is the Spirit of God and the graces of the Spirit of God working in the believer to deal with those distractions and temptations. You might compare such a believer with the soldier who is happiest when he is a war. If there are no trials, no temptations, no suffering, no persecution, they know that they are becoming stale and losing their warrior's edge. So walk down these paths. Bring them before the Lord. Even though there are temptations and distractions, this pathway is safe. You will be freed from these temptations. You are just as married to God on this path as you are anywhere else.

There are so many false fears that trouble the soul but should not.

If you are frightened by these weaknesses, you are distracted—perhaps even to the point of giving up a spiritual life.

Now let us hear from

John of the Cross

on this matter of distractions

In your spiritual exercise there will be moments of distractions and temptations. You may even come to a point of feeling dirty because of what your mind has wandered off to while you are praying. You therefore feel unworthy, and thoughts of failure come in strong. Some give up the adventure of prayer in their lives because of this.

Some have even testified that their mind wanders off to fleshly things when trying to pray more often than at any other time. Take note of these tricks. Do not consider them as having any value. Persist. Be careful especially when you are depressed. This I would call a dark night of the soul, but this is necessary for purification. These distractions do not decrease God's love for you. On the contrary, this can only increase the graces of God within you. You do realize that once you recognize these distractions and see that they are taking you away from God, you will remember His love and you will turn back to Him. The distractions will decrease. The graces will increase. You will recognize that the graces of God and the love of God are increasing and strengthening within your soul, and love of the world will grow cold. Remember that His Spirit is stronger than your flesh. Love in the senses remains in the senses. Love which comes from the Holy Spirit, remains is the Spirit of God and makes the human spirit grow and strengthen.

We turn now to

Nicholas of Jesus-Maria

Again I will remind you that Nicholas quoted many Roman Catholics who have been sainted by the Catholic Church. Here are quotes that he has given to us of great Christians who came before us. He quotes Saint Gregory who lived during the sixth century.

112

Even when a Christian has a strong spirit there can be attacks upon him. Images of sinfulness do come into the mind. The prick of the flesh suddenly wounds the soul and grieves the spirit. Heaven and earth are tightly knit together. The spirit is illuminated as it touches God and it is dimmed by temptation. This is a progressive journey.

In the presence of lustful thinking, be patient and also be tolerant, even if you feel this is something shameful. Light comes from heaven. Hell is full of darkness. But the spirit receives both as light. One accomplishes one thing in the life of the believer, the other accomplishes yet something else.

Nicholas also quotes Saint Jerome. In my prayer life very often I am walking through portholes and galleries. I am carried away by improper thoughts. I endure things which are shameful to talk about.

Here also Saint Diadoche. It can be seen that the mind can think of things proper and improper at the same instant. A man can be cold and warm at the same moment. Unfortunately for man, he has the knowledge of good and evil . . . both at the same moment. Do not struggle with these temptations.

Saint Catherine of Sienna: We have to endure improper thoughts even in communion. One day the Lord spoke to Catherine saying, "What are you so sorry about? If this afflicts you, I am here with you."

I also quote John of Jesus-Maria. It is a constant teaching among theologians that when something improper enters the mind, there is no sin as long as one ceases what he is thinking.

Saint Gregory: The one who stands more in the presence of God than others is also more tempted. The deeper one goes into the Lord, the more these distractions. This keeps the soul of the believer from becoming proud. This is a humbling experience and the person becomes tender toward others who share space on this fallen earth.

Perhaps it is Job who said it best: "No one but God can help the spirit." God sometimes leaves those whom He loves. God helps believers by going to them. He then puts them to a test by withdrawing the sense of His presence from them. They are greatly troubled. So the wise man said, "God has specially chosen me. He will make me tremble and He will test me."

Benedict of Canfield

To contest and fight against distractions will only make them stronger and leave an imprint on your spirit. Certainly do not seek to rationalize or to understand what is happening. The more the mind fights against its thoughts, the more they are remembered. Another reason not to fight against these thoughts: the more the soul is active, the more one is taken away from the presence of the Lord. The more we act, the more we exist. It is better to turn away and ignore the thoughts and distractions, and abandon oneself to life and light. Being annihilated the thoughts will fade away. The same abyss which annihilates the person also drowns distracting thoughts. No difference must be made between feeling and non-feeling. We must remain firm and assured in nothingness and leave the whole fight to God.

From the Author of
The Mystical Day

When a Christian is enjoying peace and then is tormented by his lower instincts, he must be careful not to consent to the troubled senses, but have only contempt for them. He must feed his peace as much as he can. There are believers who are much troubled when their lower part crosses the sweet peace of their will. Saint Theresa was one of them. Sometimes she used to say, "I would like to die since I cannot help this changeability of thoughts." But we must not take notice of this lower part which is nonsense, because it prevents us from keeping and from strengthening the peace. Since the loss of that peace will be bad for the soul, and the pleasantness one feel in that kind of peace is so great, we therefore must not be troubled by unwanted thoughts. That is why Theresa gives us a good piece of advice. The will, she says, being in peace, must not be bothered by thoughts or by imagination because we will be hindered by worrying.

That is why the first piece of advice that I give you is to have nothing but contempt for the senses. Firstly, because as Saint Theresa says, the senses are mad. A mystical theologian gives us another reason: We must not take any notice of them, he says, as one who has nothing to do with taste, if the believer is enjoying God. I would say more: I insist on a third reason, that not only the senses have nothing to do with enjoying the presence of God and the peace of the will, but they are completely against that peace and a great enemy of it. Therefore, you must not take any notice of them. Fourthly, nothing annoys the flesh more, nor blunts its attacks more, than contempt. Fifthly, contempt is the general remedy advised by the masters of spiritual life, and in this, as in every other thing. Saint Theresa says so when she talks about this kind of prayer. Therefore, since this torment and agitation of the lower part doesn't take away from us a taste for peace and quietness, what are we worried about? The temptation can go on as long as it will. It is enough for us to be assured that God allows it to test our patience.

The second piece of advice I am giving you is not to try too hard to drag the physical senses back to the right path, because the effort you will have to make in order to appease the senses can only cause you harm at that stage for several reasons. Firstly, it is useless because the senses are not ruled by reason.

Secondly, seeing that it is useless to try, you will worry, believing that the sensual troubles will prevent you from enjoying sweet peace. This worry is a bad thing for the prayer of peace. To try to keep enjoying God will take a great deal of care. You will find it very difficult to deal with these two things, and thus you will be crushed by the weight.

The third reason is that the attention you give to the senses diminishes the attention you should give to the peace.

The Christian will lose, says Saint Theresa, what the Lord gives him, without any effort at all. And in his inner self the reason for which the flesh thus torments and crosses his will is that the intellect cannot understand what the spirit wants. (When Theresa says the intellect, she means the imagination, because she confuses those two things. She states somewhere else that the intellect is ashamed to see that it does not understand what the believer's spirit wants, and thus it causes trouble.) The spirit is so much in God that the worry created by the intellect disturbs it very much. That is why you must not worry, for it would make you lose what you enjoy. You must let all that go and abandon yourself between the arms of love. His Majesty will teach you what you must do at that moment. All it means is that you must think yourself unworthy of so great a Good, and so must give thanks.

It often happens that someone wanting to save another one from drowning actually drowns with him and loses the life that he wants to save. The same thing happens to the believer who wants to drag the senses to the point of peace and quiet, but instead gets drowned with them in the waters of care, losing his precious peace.

If your thoughts flow into irrelevant things, you must laugh at them as if they were mad, and remain in the peace and quietness. Theses things will come and go, and you don't need to intervene.

Because the senses will become peaceful by themselves, they cannot go on forever with their rebellion against their queen. When the bees start flying, if their queen does not start flying with them, they will soon go back. They cannot live without her. The same thing will happen with our senses when they lose themselves in a thousand directions and fancies. If the spirit keeps its peace, enjoying the sweet honey of the hive, these troublesome bees will seek their mistress without whom they cannot be at peace.

The first benefit you could enjoy from the disorder of the senses would be an indomitable strength in order to keep your peace against distraction. They will become unable to change your preference for the peace that comes with the presence of God.

The kind of prayer tormented by the flesh is better and more precious in the eyes of God than prayer that never dealt with such torments. When you are troubled with these passions, and forgetting about them you can return to your inner self with peace and without care, you learn to remain at peace, even when the flesh causes trouble and deprives you of the sweet milk of peace. When you are dry, you must remain sweet and peaceful, not caring for theses passions or imagination, just as when God gives peace and joy. And this is not a small gain.

17

EXPERIENCE

I give my view on Experience in my book
A Short and Simple Way to Pray

For those who find it difficult to believe that it is easy to find God this way and who do not believe what they are told about it, they should try and experience what I have written and judge for themselves. They will see that we have told them very little about it in comparison with what it is.

I don't pretend to have more elevated feelings than others, but I am simply describing the experience that I have had and that others have had. People will become even more certain of the truth of what I say if they try and experience it.

It is Your work, oh Lord, oh Love incarnate, oh silent Word, to make other people love You, appreciate You, and hear You. The language of love is barbaric to those who do not love.

I turn your attention to
Theresa

It is important that your adviser be prudent. I mean to say that he must be able to give good advice and he must be experienced. If he fulfills those two conditions, and he is well-educated as well, it is all to the good. But if these three cannot be found together, the two first ones are most important.

It is wrong to believe that the years will make us understand what we can only know through experience. Those who have no experience of the Lord Himself believe that it must happen a certain way, and that they must become aware of it—more clearly aware of it than I express it here. But this is not something that can be simulated or imagined, since we cannot acquire it with all our efforts.

I am ready to follow what people who know a lot about theology will tell me: for although they have no experiences of these things, they have some special knowledge. God has chosen them to enlighten His church when a truth must be proclaimed. He lets them know about it, so that everybody receives this truth. If they are not dissipated or dissolute, but are servants of God, they never will be amazed by His greatness, for they know well that His power stretches further. Finally, although some things are not specifically written, theologians find comparable passages in the Scripture through which they can see that these spiritual experiences may exist. I have often seen this happen. I have also met lots of theologians who do not really know things and are easily offended. They have done me much harm.

John of the Cross

As far as this way is concerned, at least for the most elevated way and even the median way, the believer will have great difficulty to find an able and gifted guide with all necessary qualities. This counselor must be wise, discreet and experienced. If this spiritual guide has no experience with sublime states, he will be incapable of showing the Christian the way, even if called by God, and he could do a lot of harm.

Nicholas of Jesus-Maria

This man, Nicholas, extensively quotes many Roman Catholics who have been sainted by the church. Here are quotes he has given us of great Christians who have come before us.

Spiritual wisdom is different from all the sciences, because we must experience it ourselves before we understand what we are talking about. Here practice comes before theory. This wisdom is a different theory—different from any speculative wisdom. It surpasses all our ability to understand. And because some wise men and doctors of theology never reach this stage of spiritual experience, they laugh at this very high wisdom. Consequently, in this they fight against God, the sovereign giver of this wisdom. I beg those who will look at this book not to show it to these ignorant philosophers nor to doctors of theology who lead a carnal life. If those who laugh at this wisdom ever happen to know it by experience, they will approve all that is said by the mystics with the knowledge born of experience.

The subject of this book is the holy Love which must not be judged through words and through the tongue. It can be judged only through its truths. If someone wants to reach the state I have described he must love. Otherwise, the one who does not love will approach vainly to understand or to read this song of love, because an icy heart cannot understand the words that are afire. In the same way as one does not know Greek will not understand those who speak it, the language of love will sound barbaric to the one who does not love.

From the author of
The Mystical Day

It is not through human science that one can reach mystical theology, which is without forms and without images. That is to say, it teaches the kind of prayer which is without thought and without any action apart from dark quietness.

Nobody says mystics can understand the secrets of mysticism through science, or through the subtle ways of the intellect, or by any exercise, whatever it may be. Experience will lead those whom God has decided to bring to this stage. This wisdom, some others say, is not of this earth but of heaven. It has nothing to do with beautiful well-arranged words, but it concerns the reality of the Holy Spirit. This wisdom does not come from the subtleties of the intellect but from the purity of life. It will be in vain that you will look through books if you do not try to experience reality. It does not come from science, but from experience without which no one will understand. As with any secrets of love, if one does not experience them one will not understand them.

Gerson: With the knowledge that we have through faith that God is desirable and loving, our spirit and love will be led to experience our Lord without studying books, if our spirit is enlightened and quickened.

18

VISIONS AND GIFTS

I turn your attention to

Theresa

As for myself, I am amazed at the fact that the Christian who has reached this stage finds that all the raptures are taken from him except for a few occasions. What I call raptures being taken from him is loss of the senses and of warmth of exterior effects. In truth raptures are not taken away since in the innermost part they rather increase. Raptures cease in the way I have told you, and the believer does not have to endure any longer such violent ecstasies and flights of the spirit. If it still happens sometimes, it is rare; and it hardly ever happens in public as before, and in the way the believer had gotten used to it happening. And however much one gives oneself to devotional exercises it has no violent effects as it often did before. Before, if the person was looking at a religious painting or was listening to a sermon, he might become anguished and agitated. Everything frightened him and made him take flight. Now, this great weakness which before was very hard to endure and from which the person had not yet been freed comes to an end—either because his soul has found its peace or because he has seen so many things that he is not astonished anymore, or because he does not feel lonely since he enjoys the Lord's company or that of brothers and sisters, or for whatever reason after our Lord has started to show what there is in His house. This is the result of our Lord having given more strength.

John of the Cross

Of these supernatural experiences, some are from the body, others are spiritual. Those from the body are of two kinds. Some are communicated through the exterior tangible senses; others through inner physical senses. Among the latter are included all that concerns the imagination.

The spiritual ones are also of two kinds. One is distinct and special; the other is confused, obscure and general. In the distinct and special one, there are four particular ways of apprehending which are communicated to the spirit without using any bodily senses: that is to say, visions, revelations, spiritual words and emotions. General spiritual communication consists in one only: that is to say, very deep silent fellowship with God. You get to the last stage by going through all the previous stages.

Now we must know that although things may be experienced or felt in the outward senses, we must never be assured they are God's way. We should run away from these outward experiences without trying to examine whether they are good or bad. The more our impressions are exterior and have to do with the body, the more it is doubtful that they come from God, who generally communicates with the spirit, where there is more profit, than to the senses which bring with them danger and deceit. In the latter, the corporal sense becomes judge of spiritual things, thinking they are as the person feels them, although there is as much difference between spiritual things and physical senses as there is between body and soul or between sensuality and spirit.

Bodily experiences and imaginations are exterior although they may be used inside, because of the great distance and the little proportions that exist between body and soul. Although these bodily experiences sometimes communicate with the spirit, and may come from God, they are still a lot less than if the same things were more interior and spiritual. And thus those bodily things are more easily the cause of deceit, of presumption, and of vanity. Being so tangible and material, they have a strong effect on the senses, and they also seem to affect a person's judgment so that he loses his way and does not achieve his goal, which is to reach union with God.

Furthermore, the person who sees himself with these extraordinary gifts or experiences may conceive the idea that he is already *something* before God, which destroys humility and may insinuate in the soul a hidden complacency and satisfaction with itself. These experiences might include letting the person see holy and beautiful lights, letting him hear flattering words, letting him smell pleasant scents and taste sweet things, and letting him touch delights. We should always reject these figures and feelings: for although some of them come from God, it is not wrong to reject them. If they are from God, you will eventually receive the fruit that God wants to give you through them even though you rejected them.

Even if outward experiences come from God, you should not concentrate too much on these exterior emotions and visions. If the believer wishes to accept them there are six drawbacks. The first, the perfection of conducting oneself by faith diminishes, since the things one experiences through the senses do not build faith. Faith, as it has been said, is above the five senses and above material experiences. If one does not renounce these things, this is bad for the spirit since the person takes too much notice of them instead of flying towards the invisible. This is the reason our Lord said to His disciples that He had to go away in order for the Holy Spirit to come. In the same way, He did not let Magdalene touch His feet after the resurrection so that all these things would be strongly established in faith. It is because the believer does not follow the path of true resignation and abandonment that he loses contact with the spirit—that he loses the graces and blessings of God—because he tries to appropriate them and does not use them as he should. That is to say, he does not accept them properly but tries to profit by them. That would be to accept them only to find in them what one likes.

It is thus clear that these visions of the senses cannot serve as a means to achieve divine union, since they have little to do with God. So I say that from all these imaginary apprehensions and visions, and any other shape or form, whether evil or true, the believer must never bother with them. He should not even consider them, if he wants to be detached, bare, pure and simple—a condition that is needed in order to reach divine union.

That is why, to reach this perfect union with God, the believer must be very careful not to use props nor to cling to these imaginary visions nor shapes, nor figures, since they cannot help, and, on the contrary, they will hinder spiritual growth.

To help you toward being able to recognize a vision that may perhaps be from God, I offer a few principles.

The first is from Saint Paul, who says that the things that come from God are well-arranged. The second is from the Holy Spirit in the Book of Wisdom, where He says that He arranges things sweetly. The third is from theologians who say that God moves everything properly. Now it is obvious through these principles that God, in order to touch the believer and raise him from his extreme lowness to His extreme greatness and into His divine union, arranges these things in an orderly fashion. Hence God, in order to raise the believer to know God Himself must start at the lowest degree, through the senses of the body and soul, in order to raise him to spiritual understanding which has nothing to do with the senses or imaginations.

About these visions one cannot be as brief as one would like. The reason I am saying so much on this subject is because some spiritual masters think visions are good and come from God and are to be shared to help others. They are wrong, showing what Jesus Christ meant by this phrase: "If a blind man leads another blind man they both fall in the pit." He does not say they *will* fall, but *they fall*. It is not necessary for them to make a mistake in order to fall. The very presumptuousness of leading one another is already a mistake, thus they fall at least in doing that.

Although the visions and words of God are always true and certain, our way of conceiving and understanding them is not always clear and correct. This is for two reasons: One is our defective way of understanding. The other is our natural tendency to receive God's communications to us as being threatening and conditional, as if He were saying: "If these matters are not corrected. . . ." This is not God's way. The words of Christ are absolute and without condition. God says to Abraham, "I will give you this land." And to Jacob, "Do not fear, Jacob, and go to Egypt; I will go with you, and when you leave there, I will help you and lead you." This did not actually happen to them if we take it in our way of understanding. But God's immense revelations are often different in concept and purpose from what we understand them to be.

We can see that while the words of Revelation are God's words, we must not rely inflexibly on our interpretation of them, because we can easily be wrong about the way we understand them. They represent an abyss and the depths of the spirit. And although they are full of meaning, man does not understand them. As Saint Paul says, "The mind of man does not know the things that are in the Spirit of God. They are madness to him, and he cannot understand them because they are spiritual, but the spirit judges of everything." On the other hand, God sometimes speaks clearly, without making any condition, as he did to the Ninivites, to whom He prophesied that they would perish at the end of forty days.

God sometimes answers prayers that are not to the ultimate good of the believer. You could say to me, perhaps, "If this is true, why does God answer our prayer?" God adapts Himself to the weakness of the Christian who wants to follow this path. He answers in order to avoid disorienting the immature believer to the extent that he might go backwards, or for fear that the Christian might think God is angry with him when He does not answer the prayer. Such disappointments or fear might lead the weak Christian to temptation.

A father of a family has several different kinds of meat on the table, some more delicate than the others. One of the children wants to have what is in the dish nearer to him, which happens to be his favorite, although it is not the best for him. The child asks for it and the father sees that he if gives him some of the better food he will not want it. The child is determined to have what he wants, which is to his taste. Afraid that the child may go without food and feel unhappy, the father gives him what he wants, though he does not want to do so. This is as God did for the children of Israel when they asked Him for a king. He gave them a king against His will, because this was not what they needed.

Therefore this preference, this inner taste which the Christian has for gifts and blessings, is granted. Perhaps more than before, as the Christian desires them more and more. That is because the purer the Christian becomes, the more he can enjoy the spiritual gifts. Eventually, these sensitive parts would become weak and incapable of the higher things of the spirit. It follows that those Christians, because of the blessings they receive, may have to suffer some pain and weakness, consequently hampering the work of the Spirit. This Christian is not very strong nor very intense, nor as spiritual as he needs to be if he is to reach union with God. And hence come the raptures, the ecstasies, the breaking up of bones, things which always happen when communications are not purely spiritual. That is to say they are not for the spirit only, as the communications of those who have reached perfection are. These people do not have any more of these raptures and bodily torments. They enjoy freedom of the spirit without the senses taking offense. People who have been dependent on spiritual gifts and blessings may have to enter a "night of the spirit."

John of the Cross said that a believer must enter the second night of the spirit to reach divine union. There he will bare the senses and spirit of all these visions and gifts. He must walk forward in pure blind faith, which is the proper way through which he might be united to God. As he says in Osee, "I will marry you in faith, that is to say, I will be united to you in faith."

Such a strong experience as the dark night of the spirit cannot be endured in the flesh, for in fact there is no strength in the body to suffer so much without weakening.

Queen Esther, having seen King Ahasuerus on his throne clothed in royal splendor with gold and gemstones, trembled so much to see him looking so majestic that she fainted. She admits she was afraid of his glory and he seemed to her as an angel of God, his face full of graces. Her heart was very moved and troubled because glory oppresses the one who looks at it. So a believer seeing the glorified Christ should feel faint even more, because the One he knows is not an angel, but God Himself, with His face full of graces, with a terrible power and glory.

Of the voice of the Lord, Job says that it is strong: "Since as soon as we have heard a very small bit of His message, who would be able to look at the thunder of His greatness?" And somewhere else: "I do not want to discuss things with Him face to face because I am afraid that I may be oppressed by the weight of His greatness."

A person who has learned to meet God deep in his spirit, not in outward prayers, will not come to any harm nor feel the kind of pain that would be felt by one who is not prepared to see God. But the main thing is that God shows Himself kind and loving. He shows His greatness and glory to the believer, in order to prove His love and to raise him towards Himself. In the same way He favors and strengthens the believer, protecting his frail nature, showing the greatness of His Spirit with love and sweetness. This is easily done by the One who kept Moses on His right side to show him His glory. And thus the believer, finding God, has much sweetness and love, as he sees power, sovereignty and greatness, because in God all are one.

Why is it that delight and protection are strong in sweetness and love? The Christian becomes strong in order to show his delight, so that he tends to be rather strong and powerful instead of in a swoon or fainting. If the queen fainted, it was because the king did not show himself favorable to her in the beginning. His eyes were blazing and fiery. He showed her how furious he was. Later on he showed her favor and drew out his scepter, touching her and setting her aglow. She awoke after he told her that he was her brother and that she must not fear.

The King of Heaven comes at first to the believer as Bridegroom and Brother, so the believer does not fear. God shows sweetly and not furiously the strength of His power and the love of His kindness, and He communicates to her strength and love. Leaving His throne to go toward her as the Bridegroom does to His bed, where He is hidden, He bends towards her, He touches her with the scepter of His majesty, and embraces her. There we have the kingly clothes and their perfume which are the wonderful virtues of God; the splendor of gold which is divine love; the brilliant shining of gemstones; and the faith of the Word full of grace. These fill the Bride and clothe her like a queen is clothed. Transformed by these virtues from the King of heaven, the Bride sees herself as a queen. One can truly say of the believer what David says: "The queen is next to you with clothes embroidered with gold."

Francis of Sales

You can see that the flowing of the believer into God is nothing else but a real ecstasy, by which a believer finds himself quite outside his natural self—all mixed, absorbed and engulfed in God. So it happens that those who reach this holy excess of divine love, when afterwards they come back to themselves, do not find satisfaction in earthly things. They have in their heart, as Theresa did, "What is not God is nothing to me. The Scripture says that I am living, no longer for myself, but Jesus Christ lives in me; and my life is hidden with Jesus Christ in God."

If an elementary drop of water thrown into an ocean were alive and able to speak and tell us what sort of state it would be in, wouldn't it shout with joy: "Oh mortal, I really live, but I don't live in myself! This ocean lives in me and my life is hidden in its deeps!" The believer that has flown into God does not die, but he lives without living in himself. Like the stars, without losing their light, do not shine in the presence of the sun, but the sun shines in them, and they are hidden in the light of the sun. In the same way the believer, without his life, does not live anymore, being in God, and God lives in him.

The intellect and human spirit do not much belong to each other. As the philosophers have more knowledge than love for their Creator, thus good Christians have more love for God than knowledge of Him. So an excess of knowledge is not always followed by an excess of love; neither is an excess of love always accompanied by an excess of knowledge. The ecstasy of worship, on its own, does not make us any better according to what one who had been in ecstasy up to the third stage has told us. "If I know," he said, "all the mysteries, and I have all knowledge, and I do not have love, I am nothing." Being touched by the presence of the Lord can excite the intellect, showing it marvelous things which will keep an individual raised above his natural abilities. But to give the real ecstasy of the spirit, through which the believer attaches himself only and strongly to God, this belongs only to the work of the Holy Spirit.

In fact, we have seen in our lifetime several people who themselves believed that they often experienced divine ecstasies, but at the end it was clear that these ecstasies were only an illusion. A priest who lived at the same time as Saint Augustine went into ecstasy whenever he wanted to, by singing or having other people sing some sad and lugubrious tunes. He did this only to show those who were curious about it and wanted to see the sight. But what is interesting is that his ecstasy reached such a degree that he could not feel anything when they put fire to him, and he could only feel something when he had gone back to himself. And if someone spoke with a very loud voice, he heard him as if he were far away. In this state his breathing also stopped.

Philosophers also have some kinds of natural ecstasy when then are intensely focused on higher things.

If ecstasy is more beautiful than it is good, more luminous than warm, more speculative than effective, it is gravely questionable, and it deserves that one should be suspicious of it. I don't say that it is impossible to have experiences of ravishing, to have visions, even prophetic ones, even without love. I know only too well that it is possible to have love without ever having been ravished or being a prophet. In the same way one can be ravished and be a prophet without loving the Lord. But I say that the one who, when he is ravished, is more enlightened in his spirit and is able to adore God, and able—in his will—to love God, this person must be very careful. It may be that this ecstasy is wrong and makes the spirit more proud, putting the person in the position of Saul, Balaam, Caiphe—all prophets but reprobates.

John of Saint Samson

We must know that a person at this stage is still a fair way from effectual union with God, although he is able to receive something in divine light, either for simple speculation, for the taste, or for the ecstasy. Ecstasy cannot be the end and the success of all these mystical means.

The Song of Songs

At this point, out of the Lord's love, and by union with Him, the Bride is able to bear much fruit.

God will unite Himself to me eventually, and then I will be fertile and I will produce for my Bridegroom fruits more incomparably beautiful than those that I prayed for.

The Bride becomes able to help others who are being chosen for Him, but she does not yet have the ample fruitbearing that she will later have. As a bride, she has only a germ of fecundity. As a wife, she will give more. When she has reached the happiness of being received forever in God, she becomes a nursing mother.

When fruit is borne by the believer, the Bride, her lips are like honey, which distills sweetness for others. They are not her lips, nor her words, because it is the Bridegroom who talks through His Bride; and the lips of the Bride are used to express the divine word. God says, I give you the honey and milk that are under your tongue. I Myself put this honey and this milk under your tongue, and I make you distribute them to people according to their need. The Bride is honey for those who must be won through the sweetness of comfort. She is milk for the believers who have become simple and childish. The smell of her virtues and her good works which clothe her goes everywhere like a sweet incense.

As the peel is the least part of the pomegranate's taste and nutrition, in the same way what appears outside the believer at this degree is very little compared to what is hidden. The inside is full of purest love and highest graces. All this is covered by a very common exterior. For God is pleased to hide the believer that He wants for Himself. Men are not worthy of knowing them and the angels admire and respect them in spite of their very common exterior. So all those who judge according to appearances would believe them to be of the commonest kind, although God delights in them. They are not those who shine in the world by miracles nor by extraordinary gifts. This is too little for them. God keeps them for Himself and He is jealous of them. He marks them with His seal, and He says that His Bride is the sealed fountain, whose seal He is.

But why does His seal mark His special ones? Because love is as strong as death, and jealousy lasts as long as hell. How well this puts what I am trying to say, as death takes everything from whomever it has in its grips; and love attracts everything toward the believer and hides it in the secret of a living sepulcher. The jealousy of God is as enduring as hell; it will stop at nothing to possess His Bride.

Your womb, that is to say, your spiritual fertility, is like a heap of wheat as long as it is plentiful. It germinates, grows, is fruitful, can feed like wheat does and has all its qualities; but it is surrounded by lilies as a sign of complete purity.

You have made your Bride fruitful and mother of her innumerable people. You have told your angels to guard your Bride. She will bring back great profit, to You, oh God, and to all believers.

A spiritual man must not exhibit himself at the wrong time. Otherwise he would be hindered in his naked and free introversion and fellowship with God, in which he takes his rest in the abyss of his own spirit.

A spiritual believer has discernment, but he does not always judge things which have to do with himself. He sees everything, he distinguishes everything which is in his spirit. He distinguishes as much among little thoughts as in great ones, and thinks nothing is too small. But he does not care about anything. He can see things of the spirit and even have discernment about earthly circumstantial situations. But about things that are important to himself, whether they be small or mediocre, he is not able to judge. According to this truth, the less things are important to the believer personally, the less they can be judged by him. On the other hand, when important decisions are to be made, he is able to see and distinguish them and to usually come to a good decision.

The union of plenitude is not perfect until we have reached a point of being fertile, that is, able to pour out life and light to others. At the beginning of our union with God we do not have that power. We can feel and see our simplicity inside God, and we do not want to leave Him ever. In our great simplicity we are in a position where we can continue to grow into abundance, fertility, and sharing with others. The consummation of this supreme unity and its supreme plenitude must be a unity that is productive.

The union with God that an individual has does not necessarily flow to another believer, even if they both are in an advanced stage. The loving relationship with God is very personal and unique. It is simple unity, simple love, simple delight and simple peace. It is enough for both believers to be happy in their mutual worship and illumination, which both feel and both possess.

Where faith, hope and love do not show themselves any longer as acts of the senses, the whole man is lost in the very pure land where everything is simple. There light is unutterable, and the spiritual powers are in oneness. The whole man is delighted and he has no wish to go back. He submerges himself, going deeper and deeper into God. When you get there, nothing exists anymore and nothing is done humanly anymore. The very simplicity lives by Him and for Him.

Monsignor Olier

I learned through your last letter how painful it was to read one of mine. That pained me in turn, since I had no intention other than to tell you about the marvelous presence of God in our spirits. God keeps us in such a union that in spirit our feelings are mutual, however far away we find ourselves.

How faithful God is who always wants to keep your spirit open and sensitive, because He will always live in you as He has promised. This grace is unlike any other. It is amazing, when we think how unworthy we are. This grace is allowed by our Lord to be felt inside eternally. As it has been said by the prophet: *Charitate perpetua dilexite*: "I have loved you with an eternal love."

When I am not in this world any longer, I will not stop being completely yours in Jesus Christ, who is in heaven as He is on the earth, neither will I stop being as much in the love and spirit of unity which operates in those whom He links in the communion of His divine life, and whom He unites for the glory of His Father. This creates the perfect communion of the life of the Bride and the Bridegroom. Since the time when you gave yourself to the Lord, I can assure that union will be continually renewed in you.

19

SPIRITUAL ENGAGEMENT

I have had this to say about Spiritual Engagement in

The Song of Songs

In the beginning, the embrace of the right hand is truly the engagement of the Bride, but not yet the wedding. "He will embrace me," she said. "At first He will unite me to Himself by a promise of engagement, which will assure me that He will honor me one day with marriage. And that is when He will take me and I will become one with Him, and I will have no more of faltering."

The Bride in this sweet embrace of engagement goes to sleep a mystical sleep. There she enjoys a sacred peace that she has never before enjoyed.

The engagement, or mutual promises, are made in spirit when the Bride gives herself to God and when God gives Himself completely to her, so that she will one day reach union. This is the reciprocal promise. But alas, there is still a long way to go and much suffering to endure before this so-desired union is agreed to and consummated.

If some saints or some authors have established this divine marriage at some less advanced stage than the one I am describing, the reason is that they thought the engagement was the marriage and the marriage was consummation. They did not always distinguish exactly these degrees or stages as being only the first steps to the inner way. All these souls who have been engaged believe themselves to be brides, even more understandably so because the Bridegroom Himself calls them by this name Bride.

Now turn your attention to

Theresa

It seems to me that this union does not yet reach the stage of spiritual marriage, but that it is like here on the earth when two people are to be married. One tries to establish that there are similarities between the two—that they have the same kind of values, so that they become more happy with one another. The same happens here assuming they have already agreed, and the Bride realizes how specially chosen she is because she has been given such dignity, and she is well determined to do all she can to fulfill the wishes of her Bridegroom. The Lord is happy with the agreement, and He gives the believer the grace of wishing to know Him. Then He unites Himself with her.

John of the Cross

In this spiritual stage which we have just described, you would notice a very elevated state and a union of love. After a long spiritual exercise, God usually elevates the believer. This stage is called the stage of spiritual engagement with the Word, the Son of God. When this first happens, God communicates to this person some great things about Himself. There is grandeur and majesty, and He adorns His betrothed with gifts and with virtues and clothes her with the knowledge and honor of God. It is like an engaged girl on the day of her engagement.

The Bride in this verse tells how the two give mutually to each other in this spiritual engagement. In this inner cellar they have united themselves to each other by

133

love. God gives the Bride the bosom of His love. There He teaches her the wisdom of secret things. The Bride gives herself completely to Him, keeping nothing for herself or for others, saying that she will be His forever.

20

THE DARKNESS
OF FAITH

You will find these words in my book
The Song of Songs

There are people who say this union can only happen in the next life, but I am absolutely sure that it can happen in this life. There is the difference that in this life one possesses without seeing, and in the other life one sees what one possesses.

Now, of course, seeing God is an advantage of glory which is necessary for complete consummation. But glory is not an essential in this life. One is happy as soon as one possesses God, and one can enjoy Him and possess Him without seeing Him. One can enjoy Him here in the darkness of faith without having the pleasure of seeing Him. But in the next life, one will see God clearly while having the happiness of possessing Him.

Why does the Bride ask not to be looked at in her baseness? The reason is that she is beginning to enter the stage of faith and of stripping herself of feelings. Little by little she loses the strength which formerly helped her to "do good" easily.

Let me listen to your voice. The Bridegroom, through these words, asks His Bride to come our for Him from this deep silence in which she has remained till now. In all the time of faith and of being lost in God, she has kept complete silence because she had to resolve herself into the simplicity and unity of God Himself.

Harphius

When we are in this dark cloud, which the reason cannot understand, the human spirit dies to itself and lives in God and becomes one with God. God gives us peace in Himself and fulfills us.

When the believer through love has advanced beyond all image or sight, he goes into the dark nothingness of pure spirit. God becomes present as He is, the I Am.

Benedict of Canfield

This light is a pure, simple, and naked kind of faith, helped by reason and confirmed by experience. It has nothing to do with the senses nor with any kind of human fellowship, nor with anything to do with self. This light has to do with the spirit, where it fellowships with God without any intermediaries.

I call this faith pure in order to exclude the help of the physical senses. It is no good to try and find support in them. They must be completely given up. We cannot always have the help of sentient devotion, but pure faith must always remain. One who possesses it is not assured, but is uncertain. Still this faith must be stable, even if uncertain. Our physical, mental and emotional senses are wrong and lying. They persuade us that imaginary things really exist. But this faith is true, and it annihilates the material things. If we live in the senses they will keep us in darkness. On the contrary, faith which makes us live in the spirit is full of light.

Secondly, I call this faith simple to exclude all reasoning. Reasoning is contrary to the purity of faith. Reasoning makes faith human, whereas it must be divine. Reasoning creates actions and consequently creates being and not annihilation. Reason creates images that come between God and the human spirit.

Thirdly, I say that faith must be continuous. It must be without interruption in order for us to be able to reach this abyss of nothingness and wholeness. Although it seems difficult, you can practice the presence of God continuously in your daily life.

John of the Cross

We can say about the believer who is going through these stages, that he advances unknown and is hidden from the devil. One who is happy to walk in the darkness of faith, taking faith as a guide and abandoning all natural imaginations and all natural reasoning, really progresses. The night of faith belongs to the spirit of man. This part is consequently more obscure, insomuch as it deprives him of the light of reason—or to put it better, it blinds him. And thus we can compare him to midnight which is the most intimate, and darkest, part of the night.

Theologians say that faith is a habit of the soul, dark but certain. Faith is an obscure habit because it makes us believe truth revealed by God, which is above any light of reason and above any human intellect. How does this extreme light of faith which is given to the spirit bring darkness? The most overcomes the less and deprives us of it: The light of the sun surpasses all other lights, so that other lights do not appear when the sun shines.

Faith is symbolized by the cloud which separated the Children of Israel from the Egyptians when they were about to walk into the Red Sea. The Scriptures say that it was a dark cloud which illuminated the night. It is a strange thing that being dark, the cloud was illuminating the night. This is to make us understand that faith is an obscure and dark cloud for the soul. (It is also a night, since in the presence of faith, the soul remains deprived and blinded of its natural light.) Faith, though darkness, illuminates and gives light to the darkness of the soul, so that a wise man is on the same plane with his disciple.

The man who is in darkness cannot be well enlightened by other kinds of darkness. The writer of the psalms teaches us: "Day announces news to the day, and night teaches the night, which comes after the day." The believer does not enjoy clear wisdom, and having faith is like a blind person, deprived of his natural light. So we must come to the conclusion that faith, which is a dark night, gives light to the person who is in darkness. It proves what David says: "The night will be my light and my delight." In the pleasure of my pure fellowship and union with God, the night of faith will guide me, meaning that the believer must be in darkness in order to have light, and thus be able to advance.

In Job, the Scripture says that God spoke to him in the dark air (which the darkness of faith is called, where Divinity is covered when it communicates with the believer). This darkness will have an end. The darkness will end "when what is partly got rid of," that is to say the darkness of faith, so that "what is perfect will come." That is divine light. Faith contains in itself divine light, that is to say that God is in faith. This life, when finished, interrupted by the end of mortal life, will see the light and the glory of God. It is then clear and obvious that the believer, in order to be united with God in

138

this life and to be able to communicate with Him, needs to join himself with darkness.

I have seen a person who had several conversations with God, some very true ones, and she also had some very false ones. I wonder very much what happens when such a person remembers some of these conversations and believes or supposes straight-away that her conversations are with God and says: "God told me, God answered me." It doesn't work that way. But it is what this sort of person tells herself most often. They want it to be that way so much, and this is so much in their heart, that they answer themselves and think it is God who is answering. This makes them fall into great dreams if they do not check themselves and if the one who leads them does not forbid them strictly from these kinds of things. These individuals usually get more gossip and impurity of soul than humility of spirit. They think a lot of themselves, believing that God has spoken to them. And it will be nearly nothing, because everything that does not cause humility and love, holy simplicity and silence, what worth can it be? Now I say that it can take you away from the path to divine union. For if the believer takes any notice of the fact that God may have spoken to him, it will take him away from the depths of faith.

You may ask me why the intellect must deprive itself of these truths, saying that the Spirit of God enlightens your mind, so how can it be bad. I answer that the Holy Spirit enlightens a person according to the stage of the person's growth. The Holy Spirit will not enlighten him more than in faith. The purer and more perfect the believer is in faith, the more he has the innate love of God. The more he has divine love, the more the Holy Spirit enlightens him and communicates spiritual gifts to him. And although the Holy Spirit enlightens the believer somewhat about the truth, still this truth is very different from reality. It is as must different as gold is from vile metal. And as for an abundance of light, truths could be compared to the reality of light as between a drop of water and the whole sea. In one case the wisdom of two or three truths is communicated, and in the other case the wisdom of God in general, who is the Son of God, is given to the soul by faith. If you tell me that everything is for the good and that one does not prevent the other, I will tell you that the earthly wisdom of "truths" can prevent many things if the believer takes notice of having received communication from God. It makes the believer concentrate on things of little importance, which could prevent him from reaching the stage of union in the abyss of faith, in which God secretly teaches the believer's spirit. When God teaches him in a hidden way, deep in his spirit, then the believer is uplifted without knowing the way God has done it.

The one who will be given grace and supernatural gifts must keep secret the joy of this gift. God who gives it to him supernaturally in order to help the church will push this person in a hidden way from stage to stage as the person tries to communicate with God in spirit. Jesus Christ forbade His disciples to worry about their message or which way they would express it, because it was a spiritual matter of faith.

The second drawback could come from this first one. That is to say, a believer could lose or endanger his faith. It could happen in two ways. One concerns others—trying to do miraculous things or to have extraordinary (and useless) virtues. This is tempting God, which is a great sin. Furthermore, the believer may not be successful, and thus contempt towards the faith might come from this. Failure will not always happen, though, and if the believer was successful, even then he would fail and be guilty, because he used these graces when he should not have. In other words, believers do harm to themselves as far as faith is concerned because, trying to make a big thing out of miracles, they leave the exercise of faith. Wherever there are signs and testimonies, there is not much merit in believing. That is why Saint Gregory says that there is no merit in believing when there are human and palpable proofs.

The narrow door is this night of the senses. The believer rids himself of visible proofs, perceptions and feelings in order to go through the door, being guided by faith, which is far away from any senses. In order to advance, the believer goes through this door and then out onto the narrow path of the night of the spirit. He goes into this night, advancing towards God in very pure faith. This is the way to achieve union with God. This path is very narrow, obscure and terrifying, so much so that there is no comparison between the night of the senses and the night of the spirit. It is understandable that very few people take this path; however, it is well worth it.

This dark night is an influence of God on the believer, and it purges him of the common imperfections, both natural and spiritual. God teaches the spirit secretly and instructs it in perfection of love, having nothing to do but to be attentive and loving toward God, listen to Him, and receive His light . . . without knowing how this happens. This disposes the believer to a loving union with God.

We wonder why this divine light is also called obscure night, since this light illuminates and cleanses the believer from his ignorance. There are two reasons that this divine light of wisdom is darkness for the believer. The first reason is that the elevated state of divine wisdom which must surpass the believer's stage of awareness seems darkness to him. The second reason is that the baseness and impurity of human life makes the pure light painful and distressing and obscures the blessing.

To prove the first, we must suppose a certain doctrine of the philosopher who says that the clearer and more evident in themselves divine things are, the more hidden they naturally are to man. When the light is clearer, it hurts and blinds the eye of the owl. The more you look straight at the sun, the more it causes darkness and deprives you of your vision.

Why is it that when this divine light of union with God shines in the soul which is not quite yet enlightened, it causes darkness to the believer? It causes spiritual darkness because it exceeds the believer's ability to see, and so it darkens his vision and deprives him of his natural way of understanding. The believer's natural and intellectual strength is vanquished and deprived of the common and ordinary way of understanding.

That is why David puts around God a cloud and darkness, not that it is thus in faith, but only as far as our feeble intellects are concerned, which are blinded by this immense light. Our view remains obscure, not being able to reach such a sublime state. David also says that because of His splendor the clouds have disappeared in His presence. This is why God, visiting the believer who is not yet transformed and shining on him a ray of secret wisdom, causes his intellect to be in darkness. The fact is that two contrary opinions cannot subsist in the same subject; hence the believers must necessarily be hurt and suffer. The believer is the subject where we find those two opposites, fighters and defenders, together.

The believer is well-hidden and covered with this darkness or mystery which is around God, because the believers are a tabernacle and residence to God Himself, and they are surrounded by a strong wall and perfect safety. While the believer is hidden in darkness, he is guarded against himself and all other kinds of harms. Being hidden in God from the worries of men, we are strengthened against all temptations which may come from men. Being in his tabernacle is to be engulfed in dark water where we are free from the flesh and the world. There we can surely say that we walk in darkness and in safety.

It is certain that this believer is on the right path, although in darkness. It is to strengthen the spirit that this obscure, painful and dark water of God is placed in the believer's life. The believer develops a real determination to not do anything that he knows could offend God.

Some people who have taken this path would very much like to tell their spiritual guide what is happening to them, but they do not know how; and thus they really do not want to say it, especially if their prayer has become slightly simpler so that they can hardly feel it. They can only say that their heart is happy, peaceful and satisfied, that they feel God, and as far as they know everything is going well.

It is not the same thing when the gifts that the soul receives are special ones, as for instance strong feelings, visions et cetera. These special gifts usually necessitate the participation of the senses. Theses gifts one can express, using the image of the senses. But this power to express them does not mean they are greater than deep silent fellowship with God. That fellowship can hardly be expressed so that others can understand it. This is one reason it is called secret fellowship, along with the fact that it can hide the believer who is in faith.

Sometimes such a believer is so completely absorbed in God that he knows clearly that he is forsaken by the world and is very far away from all, so that it seems to him that he has been put in a deep solitude where no human being could reach. As in an immense desert which has no limit, a delectable and pleasant desert which is very deep, very vast and very lonely, in this desert the believer feels secret and hidden. He sees himself being raised above our temporary earthly realm.

This abyss of divine wisdom so much elevates and strengthens the believer's spirit that he knows that earthly life, even with its knowledge of truths, is very low compared with knowing God Himself. This one understands that expression and words that are used to talk about divine things in this life fall short, are too low and insufficient. Although one talks about these things in the most elevated and the wisest way one can, it is impossible in natural life to have divine knowledge and divine feeling. The person who is enlightened in this truth—that is, truth that cannot be reached and even less expressed in human terms—is right to call it secret. It is a mystery.

Since the greatest wish of the follower of Christ is union with the Bridegroom, and when he sees that this union cannot be found by anything or anyone that is earthly, he must turn toward faith as someone desperate to have more light. There is only one way to reach true union with God. The believer tells the Bridegroom with great desire: "Oh faith of my Bridegroom, Jesus Christ, you will uncover now for me the brightness and the truth of my well-beloved. You have infused this truth in my spirit."

The Bride says that these truths are inscribed in her womb, that is to say, in her spirit. By her spirit, she has these infused truths through faith, although her intellectual understanding of them is not perfect. She says that they are inscribed in pencil, because a pencil or a drawing is not a perfect painting. In the same way, knowledge of faith is not something perfect. When we will see things clearly, they will be perfect and complete. The apostle says: "When what is perfect will have arrived," which is clear vision, "that which is in part will disappear." This is the knowledge of faith.

Now on this pencil drawing of faith there is another pencil drawing of love in the heart of the lover. The faith of the Bride is penciled or painted in her inner being, so that when there is union of love, the Bride lives in the Lover and the Lover in the Bride.

God can pour love on and elevate the believer without communicating or increasing intelligence. This has been experienced by several mystics. These people often see themselves burning with the love of God without having any more understanding than before. They can understand little but love a lot or can understand a lot and love less. These mystics are not proud of their intellectual knowledge of God. The spirit can drink at the fountain of love without the intellect acquiring new knowledge.

When a believer has reached such a stage, when he goes beyond the human intellect, to know God and enjoy Him in faith and in love, then one can say that this person has reached God, because he is lost to all else.

Do not say that this Christian is not progressing or that he is doing nothing. If his intellect is not expanding, then he is working his way to the spirit. But you would say this person does not feel anything distinctly? On the contrary, I say that if he understood distinctly, then he would not progress, since God is beyond all understanding and surpasses all intelligence.

The believer must get away from earthly concepts and walk in faith, believing but not seeing. This is the way to get nearer God, without understanding and thus without worry. Intelligence may make you turn back, trying to use subtle notions and other ways to understand here below. If intellect is not having its influence on you, you are progressing. And progressing means to walk more by faith. And since intelligence is incapable of understanding what God is, you will go to God without understanding.

So when you are blaming this person for not having understanding or distinct feelings, you are right. But this is useful and proper, because this person must not worry about intelligence. This person must walk in perfect faith.

Nicholas of Jesus-Maria

tells us:

Saint Bonaventure wrote the following: Without knowing anything about union with God, you will be resurrected to union with Him by your strong desire and fervent love for Him. This cannot be known through reason.

In this darkness, knowledge has no importance. You must only have a burning desire for God alone, who is perfectly unknown. Then you will be united to God, and you will see God in this darkness which is above intellect. Human intelligence, which has no eyes, could not reach and know God.

So the degrees of this love are: first, to leave behind you all things pertaining to the senses; second, to leave all those pertaining to intelligence; thirdly, to enter into the darkness where God appears.

The essential knowledge of God still remains. This knowledge of God is what Moses means is different from the knowledge men have before entering into the darkness of ignorance. Man is here as separated from himself. Through the fact that he is chosen, which leads to real knowledge, he is united to God. God is still intellectually unknown to him, but he knows a much better way than the intellectual way.

We must have spirits without eyes, because the spirit cannot look at the divine essence through intellectual eyes. We must forget about seeing. As it is written: "Do not keep your eyes on me because they make me fly away." Then Jesus Christ hides Himself from us when we try to look, with the eyes of the intellect, upon the Wisdom from above.

Harphius: Through naked knowledge the believer goes on entering into this divine darkness, where he has a perfect ignorance of God, being placed as if between two tables, to starve to death. Thus he will remain sitting down in a naked darkness, establishing immediately his residence in front of the unknown and glorious presence of God.

Abbey Gilbert: "During the night I have looked for the one that my soul loves." In order to find the Beloved, the night helps, obviously.

Gerson: Having renounced everything that can be felt or imagined or understood, the spirit goes towards love in the divine darkness where it (the spirit) is united to God.

Taulere: If God must shine inside us in a divine manner, not only our natural light will have nothing to do with it, but it must be completely annihilated. We must withdraw from everything, for in this way we can know God. Our science must become pure ignorance, and we must forget ourselves and everyone and everything. For there is nothing more useful for man than to put himself in a state of darkness and ignorance, when he leaves behind all knowledge, or rather has lost all knowledge. Jesus Christ imparts this to each of His faithfuls: Renounce your light for the love of Me, which compared to Mine is true darkness and contrary to Mine. And I, being the true light, will give you in your darkness My eternal light, My joy, My blessing, My essence and My life. Here in this immersion, all equality and inequality vanish, for in this abyss of Divinity, the spirit loses itself, not knowing anything anymore, either of God, either of itself, or equality or inequality, or of anything.

Rusbroche: When we come back to our inner selves, the fruitful unity of God seems like a darkness or like something that is completely incomprehensible. Although the air be illuminated by the splendor of the sun and although our sight is very piercing and sharp, still we cannot keep our eyes on the rays that cause this splendor and look fixedly at the sun itself. The eyes cannot do that. They perceive the splendor of the rays only indirectly and passively. In the same way the brightness of the incomprehensible light of God seems so great and appears to us with such strength that all action must cease and the self diminishes under the action of God. From this unity of God a certain quantity of simple light shines on the inner man—the light appearing as darkness, nakedness and nothingness. In the darkness man is surrounded or embraced on all sides; and losing everything, he goes as someone who has lost his way. In nakedness he has lost all consideration and all discretion of all things.

Richard of Saint Victor: Love's sweetness can be felt, but one cannot see what kind it is. There is still a cloud and darkness all around, and the throne of God is still among the clouds. In this state the believer can feel his Beloved but cannot see Him, and if he sees Him he sees Him in the night as under a cloud.

Albert the Great: The believer must rise above himself and everything that is created. He cannot see the Beloved nor imagine Him, but this gracious Lover wishes for the most intimate affection. He is not estimable nor appreciable, but He is worthy of the whole love of a pure heart. He is lovable and delectable above everything, and His kindness and perfection are infinite. And so the believer is transported into the darkness of the spirit and raised in faith, while entering deeper into his being.

Ambroise Florentin: When a Christian tries to rise to the mystical knowledge of God, leaving the images of all created things with or without a body, he hides himself in a secret cloud where there is marvelous ignorance; for here he cannot be helped by science or knowledge. That is to say, he loses all images on which the knowledge of man is based.

Angela of Foligni: I saw God in a dark obscurity, because God is beyond everything one could think of Him or conceive of Him. He is beyond everything, and He surrounds with darkness because He is very secret and very hidden.

Bartholomew of the Martyrs: The believer is being prepared to enter into the divine abyss with simplicity and joy. The eye of reason, being shocked and dazzled by seeing such a great light, takes its rest in darkness, which is the greater light in this exile.

Picus of the Mirande: In an advanced stage of progress, we go into the light of ignorance and—being blinded by the darkness of ignorance and being also blinded by the darkness of divine splendor—we shout with the prophet: "Lord I have fainted at the entrance to your residence."

John of Saint Samson

There is an indeterminate time when the joy of love consists in the unhappiness of the self. In this state the believer, paradoxically, lives very happily in total love. From then on that believer is so like God that one could never find him outside God. What am I saying? This expression of being like God is too little. Because of our human weakness, we cannot express it adequately.

I might say that being full of God the believer is completely full of Him in His infinite expansiveness and plenitude. Finally the believer can find nothing of himself, and he is engulfed in the same love which flows from unity to a love between two, and then back to unity.

It is probably hard to understand that full and complete happiness with consummated love could exist at the very same time with earthly misery. Uncreated Love is no near and yet so far, because its infinite plenitude can only be reached from an infinite distance. This life so elevated and so lost cannot be reached nor understood, for understanding is of the senses, even if it seems very spiritual.

From this point on the human intellect feels itself and sees itself completely lost in God, without ever wanting to get our of that state. And that is even in spite of the sufferings which may happen at the beginning of the experience. In all these things consists the supereminence of the life of the spirit and the blessing of the Spirit in the One who understands the believer but is not understood by the believer.

I should tell you that it is good to be of a really affectionate nature, and thus to try with deep wishes until you have been completely consumed and your active strength is annihilated, being lost in God. This is the way to enter into the true and sure peace. However, God often makes His spouse suffer, and often for a long time. But the suffering is often accompanied by light and by delicious sights, and it happens quickly in the soul, as in lightning and very light thunder. I want you to know that although all this happens with great pain and anguish, and it is felt deep in the spirit, still the delicious and bright manifestation of the Spirit makes the frequent pain at this stage tolerable and acceptable.

A scholarly theologian, once talking to a student, told him that the scholarly will learn things about their faith much more perfectly than one who is following this deeply spiritual way. Hearing this, the student was astonished, and without answering, he concluded to himself that this might be true for some people but not for him. His simple aim, beyond all faith and all science, came from love. Love beyond love completely possesses in imperceptible perception.

The Mystical Day

What is useful in mystical prayer is general knowledge of God without distinguishing between His perfections or particular characteristics. These cannot be thought about.

To understand perfectly what is naked faith, or what is its nature, we must see in which way it resembles ordinary faith and in what way it is different from it.

The first thing is that, like ordinary faith, it is divine—but it is higher. Since we are human, we can only say that it is *probably* naked faith. It might be divine or human. When it is divine it is the same sort of thing as common faith which we received in redemption. When it is human faith, it is only a belief, practice, or prayer that is agreeable to God.

The second resemblance is that these two beliefs have the same real Object, that is, God as truth.

Another difference has to do with action. That is, common faith is action. Although faith cannot really be called an action, it is usually wrapped in an action which can be seen.

An act of naked faith or mystical faith is one which cannot be seen by human

145

eyes. Naked faith has its seat in the human spirit; peace has its seat in the highest part of the will; common faith has its seat in the mind. This is because although these two kinds of belief are beyond the senses and beyond reason, mystical faith comes from an even higher place, rising well beyond any perceptible action.

Hence another difference, which is that common faith does not simplify the intellect as mystical faith does. This mystical faith denudes the intellect of any thought. That is why it is called simple and not common.

A mystical author says that the man who focuses inwardly, that is to say the one who operates without shapes and images, has the same belief as those who look for signs. However, he has something more than the others. His feelings are more elevated. A six-year-old or a theologian may see the same sign, understanding it very differently. We must say the same thing about a common Christian and a spiritual man. The second kind of man, whom this mystical author calls an elevated and hidden man, has a knowledge beyond the light and beyond all forms and images. He believes in a kind of dark and uniform simplicity, and he has an elevated experience.

The will takes part in this prayer, but the will cannot operate unless some light directs the will. This light is none other than naked faith.

21

MELTING
OF
THE SOUL

As seen in my book
A Short and Simple Way to Pray

Prayer is a warm melting of the soul, which makes it disappear and go up to God.

When one knows how to stay near Him and remain in His presence, the presence of God knows how to melt and dissolve the hardness of the believer's heart. While the heart melts, it gives up a scent to God. That is why the Bridegroom, seeing that His Bride had melted in this way as soon as her Beloved had spoken, says to her: "Who is the one who comes up from the desert like a little puff of perfume?"

Ordinary earth cannot be changed into gold. Fire must melt the gold that comes out of the earth. Then the fire must dissolve all the earthly and foreign substance that remains.

The Song of Songs

When the believer is carrying his cross, his beauty is not flawless. But after he has melted under setbacks and sorrows, he is completely beautiful.

Although the Bridegroom is hidden, He still grants graces to His friends. These graces are bigger when the hardships are longer and harder. His Bride found herself in a new situation which was good for her, but she did not know it as such. Her soul melted and liquefied as soon as her Beloved spoke. And through this melting she lost her narrow and hard traits which had prevented the consummation of the spiritual marriage.

You belong so much to your Beloved that nothing can prevent you from losing yourself in Him. Since you have been quite melted by the warmth of His love, you have been prepared to flow into Him as if this was your very purpose.

The Beloved found His Bride all melted in Him and quite prepared for the consummation of the marriage, to be received in Him forever.

I turn your attention to
Theresa

When I was thinking about what to write, our Lord said to me these words: "My daughter, your life melts in order to enter into Me perfectly. It is not you that lives anymore, but I myself live in you. You cannot understand all this. It is as if when you seem to be understanding, you don't understand anything."

Nicholas of Jesus-Maria
tells us:

Saint Bernard said: Oh, holy and chaste love! Oh, sweet and pleasant affection! Our clear intention of the will is pure and clear when there is nothing of itself. Even more pleasant and sweet because everything we feel is divine! A small drop of water mixed with lots of wine seems to get lost completely, taking the taste and the color of wine. A red hot poker becomes just like fire itself, having been deprived of its proper and original shape. Air lit and penetrated by the light of the sun transforms itself into light, even to the point of being illuminated. At this stage all human affection is melted into God and forgets its own personality. It becomes completely absorbed in the will of God.

Francis of Sales

The heart of the Savior, true oriental pearl, unique and of inestimable worth, was thrown into a sea of bitterness on the day of His passion. He was resolute, and He melted in His pain.

Love stronger than death makes the heart melt much more quickly than all other passions. My soul, says the Bride, melted as my Beloved was talking. What does this mean, it melted? It means it was not contained in itself anymore but it melted toward its divine Lover.

God ordered Moses to talk to the rock so that it should produce waters. So it is nothing extraordinary if God Himself makes the soul of His lover melt when He talks to her sweetly.

Balm is by nature neither fluid nor flowing; and the longer it is kept the harder it gets; and finally it becomes red and transparent. Even so, heat dissolves it and makes it fluid.

Love made the spouse fluid and flowing, which the Bridegroom calls spilt oil. Now she says that she is all melted with love. "My love," she says, "flowed when my Beloved spoke to me." The love of her Spouse was in her heart like a powerful new wine which cannot be kept in its barrel, for it spills everywhere. The Bride follows her love, and says of Him, "Your breasts are better than wine spilling, or precious perfumes." She adds, "You have my flowing oil."

And as the Spouse had spilt His love in the heart of the Bride, reciprocally the Bride pours her love in the heart of the Bridegroom. And as we can see that a hill touched by strong rays seems to comes out of itself and change its shape to flow toward the place where the rays come from, it is the same way the soul of this lover flows towards the voice of her Beloved, coming out of herself and out of the limits of her natural being, in order to follow the One who is talking to her.

But how does this sacred melting of the Bride into the Beloved happen? An extreme willingness of the lover towards what she loves produces a certain spiritual powerlessness, which results in the fact that she feels she cannot stay within herself. This is why, as a melted balm which has neither firmness nor solidity, the Bride lets herself go towards her Lover. She does not throw herself into this union, but she goes toward her Lover flowing, like something fluid and liquid, towards the Divinity that she loves.

We can see the clouds, thickened by the wind of noon, melt and become rain, unable to remain in themselves, and they fall and flow towards the earth, mixing intimately with the earth they humidify, so they become only one thing. But the Bride, although a lover, still remains in herself. Then she gets out from this sacred flowing and holy fluidity and leads herself not only to be united with the Beloved but to mingle with Him. You can see then that the flowing of a believer toward God is nothing but real ecstasy in which the believer is completely outside of his usual state, all mingled, absorbed and engulfed in his God.

22

FREE CHOICE
AND
LIBERTY

God gives us our complete freedom, and it is an error to believe we are not free. As freedom is the only thing that God has given us personally, the most pleasant sacrifice that we could give to Him is the sacrifice of our free choice. One gives it to Him a long time before He accepts it, but when He has accepted it He becomes master of the way we behave and makes us move as He likes. Love is always free, because it is given freely; and the believer finds that this happy slavery, from which he cannot nor does not want to escape, is perfect freedom. On the other hand, the freedom a man holds to himself is a hard slavery.

I have talked a lot in what I have written about liberty and the giving of this liberty to God, and also how to act when that freedom has been given away. When one has explained oneself once, one must not always try to explain oneself again, in particular when one writes quickly; so here I have only said a few words about freedom of choice.

A Short and Simple Way to Pray

There is a difference in choice that is freely given. Steam attracted by the sun is not given freely and does not follow willingly, as does the believer who, given freedom of choice, follows his Lord. God is like a very strong magnet, but it is an attraction that the believer follows freely. Being equally strong and sweet, He attracts by His strength, and wins through the sweetness of His grace.

Francis of Sales

Our Lord attracts our hearts to Himself by the pleasures He gives us. These pleasures make us aware of His sweetness. But before this sweetness has taken and tied us by its bonds which make us willing slaves with perfect consent, God exercises His kindness toward us, and He continues to do so. We remain completely free in our choice to consent to celestial attractions or to reject them.

Oh! Lord Jesus, when will it be that, having sacrificed everything, we shall sacrifice for You all that we are! When will we offer our free will to you in sacrifice, our free will, the only child of our spirit? When will it be that we will tie it and make it lie down on the pyre of Your cross—of Your thorns, of Your spear—so that like a small lamb it is a pleasant victim of Your good pleasure, to die and to burn from fire and from the blade of Your holy love? Oh, free choice of my heart, how good it will be to be tied and spread on the cross of the divine Savior! How hopeful it is for you to die to yourself, to burn forever as a sacrifice to the Lord!

My free choice is never so free as when it is enslaved by the will of God. It is never so enslaved as when it is used by my own will. It is never more alive than when it dies to itself, and it is never so dead as when it lives for itself.

We have the freedom to "do good" or "do bad," but if we choose bad it is not to use but to abuse this freedom of choice. Let us renounce this unhappy freedom, and let us become slaves and attach our freedom of choice to celestial Love. Let us become slaves of Love. Slaves of love are happier than kings!

Benedict of Canfield

After this stage of spiritual destitution comes the fourth and last stage, that is, the nearness of His person, which is nothing else than a continual presence and a habit of union between God and His Bride. In this union the believer is clothed with God and God with the believer. Without interruption they are together, for whoever remains in divine love remains in God and God with him.

A Short and Simple Way to Pray

A really humble person is not surprised at his weaknesses. The weaker he is, the more he gives himself to God. God only is great, and He is honored only by those who are humble. And destroying our own being proclaims the sovereign being of God. We must cease to be, so that the Spirit of the Word should be with us.

I turn your attention to
Thomas A. Kempis

God protects and gives freedom to those who are humble. He loves them and comforts them; He lowers Himself towards them; He grants many graces to them; and after the humble have been for a long time in a low position, God raises them to sovereign glory. God confides His secrets to those whose hearts are humble. He invites them and attracts them to Himself. Those who have humble hearts will remain in peace in everything that could cause confusion or shame, because the world is nothing to them and they trust only in God.

Catherine of Genoa

A mind which has been humbled sees, hears and feels these great secrets and soon reaches divine union.

Those who want to see straight spiritually must pull out the eyes of presumption, for pride blinds those who want to know everything with their own intellect. A humble intellect is soon enlightened, but a proud intellect without wisdom will never reach union with God.

A heart which is with God, enthroned with Him, can see all the creation below him, but not through pride or through greatness. It is simply because he is united with God, and because of this union it seems to him that wherever God is, he is also; and whatever is God's is also his own.

Theresa

As for humility, it must always be foremost, so that we know that no powers come from us. We must know, however, what kind of humility this must be.

Humility does not cause us to worry about what we say, fearing it will seem to be to our own praise. Humility knows that the lord of the garden produces the fruit. It is not the fruit itself that does it. If a humble believer says anything about faith, it is for the glory and divine majesty of God. The believer knows that his faith is not of himself; and even if he wanted to he could not ignore speaking of his faith.

(I think great damage is done to Christians who pray a lot. They are prevented from advancing toward union with God because they have a false feeling of virtue.)

It does not hurt us to consider heavenly things and the glory of God. On the contrary we rejoice in it, and considering and seeing all this we try to reach a higher state. We can endure what happens in this place of exile if such a great God communicates with us and we see that in His great goodness and mercy He cherishes us. Anyone who is offended by hearing that God gives His grace in this place of exile must not have humility or love for his neighbor. How could we not rejoice that God should grant these graces to our brothers!

One could say that these things are impossible and that we should not defraud the weak. But I say that it is better to show the unbelievers these things, which are indeed true, than to fail believers by not teaching them that God grants these graces.

John of the Cross

The believer could not reach these kinds of ideas through any of his own imagination. God brings these spiritual things into the believer's inmost being apart from the believer's own ability. Whence is it that sometimes when the believer is hardly thinking about such things, his divine Majesty gives him these divine contacts. Moreover, these bits of knowledge are given suddenly to the believer and without his trying to get them. The believer does not have to wish for them or pretend to get them, but he only has to be humble and full of resignation. God will do this when He wants and whichever way He pleases.

I don't believe that we must try to reach these things. Rather, they are part of the union, which we do try to reach. That is why we teach you to part with everything and to detach yourself from everything, in order that God should grant His graces: His humility, and suffering for His love with resignation and without hope of reward. Moreover, these favors are not given to attach to material possessions, because these favors are usually caused by a very special love that God has for believers who love Him with a very pure love and with a very disinterested heart.

This is what the Son of God wanted to say to Saint John. "Whoever loves Me will be loved by My Father, and I will love him and I will appear to him." This is the kind of account and contact we are talking about.

Beginners feel very fervent and diligent about spiritual things and devotional exercises. However, because of their imperfections they sometimes feel a kind of secret pride which gives them some satisfaction about themselves. In this way they resemble the Pharisee who, while he praised God, was very proud of the things he had done and held the publican in contempt. Presuming too much about themselves, they usually talk a lot but do not do much. At times they want to show their spirituality and devotions, and in order to do this they make an exterior show of themselves with sighs and other ceremonies. At times they pretend to have visions, in public rather than in secret. They take pleasure when people get angry about the very thing they desire most of all.

Some of them try to get into the good graces of their spiritual guides. They find it difficult to confess their sins directly and clearly, being afraid that others might have contempt for them. They distort their sins in order not to seem so bad. They find excuses so as not to accuse themselves.

These vulnerable Christians strengthen themselves to go further in humility. They not only have contempt for their actions but, not being happy with themselves, they think others are much better than they are. They envy them, wishing to be able to serve God as the others do.

Because they are full of fervor, they do good works and like doing it. They walk in humility more and more, knowing that God is worthy; and they consider what they are doing for God to be very little.

If they naturally have calmness and humility, they have a great desire to be instructed by someone who can help them on their way. And thus, they would rather talk with those who don't think much of their spirit and of their state: that is, those who have a simple spirit, pure and true, which is very agreeable to God.

Since wisdom inhabits these humble souls, it makes them hide their treasure inside and chase out evil. It is a grace that God gives to those who are humble, together with other virtues. And this grace God denies to those who are proud. These people would give the blood of their hearts to whoever is a servant of God, and would help him as much as they can to do the right thing. When they think they fall into imperfections, they will bear themselves with humility and living fear of God, and they will go on hoping in Him. But I know there are not many Christians who, from the beginning, walk this way. That is why, as we are going to show, God allows the dark night, as He wants to purify from imperfections.

The believer gets out of the dryness and emptiness of this night with spiritual humility, which we have said is spiritual pride. Through this humility the believer obtains knowledge of self, gets rid of all these imperfections he used to fall into before. Considering himself so miserable, he cannot think that he walks more perfectly than others nor that he is more advanced than others. Far from it, he recognizes that others are more advanced than he is. Finally all the imperfections that come with spiritual pride are taken from him.

John of Saint Samson

Humility is not natural to men, but to God alone, who chose to be clothed in it, so that those who would never reach perfect love should at least become humble and should humiliate their arrogance in the humility of the eternal Word made man.

Those who are strongly touched and full of divine wisdom admit no humility for themselves nor in themselves. Those who are assured in their inner spiritual being of the abundance of God's life-giving love are so full of God that they see plainly the nothingness of everything and their own nothingness. Humility in itself is only a way to get to nothingness. Nothingness is their aim, and in order to get to it they use humility and humiliations without thinking about humility nor humiliations.

That is the way Wisdom builds its house, and the believer, being host to this divine Wisdom, receives it with a mutual and reciprocal pleasure. Love and virtue build this house, this vessel or, to put it better, this temple which Wisdom must inhabit. It is not through a number of good works that one builds this divine construction. It is infinite Love which continues to love its object in whatever way possible. And humility goes with it.

Humility always goes with love. They are both together in the service of God. Now it can happen that a man should become so completely humble that he does not know anymore what humility is, nor any other virtue, even love. He becomes above it, in God, in an ineffable way. In fact, as soon as there is nothing in man of man, he is then the instrument of God, and can without thinking continue forever to do God's holy will.

I come back to the nothingness of myself and many others. It is God who acts through me. Love and virtue are apart from me, or to put it another way, they do not exist for me anymore. Where I am and where I live there are no more any differences nor distinctions.

Humility exists only in Jesus Christ and is to be exercised only in Him. When you are insulted, accept these insults with all your heart. Do not reflect on yourself because that would be forgetting your Lord. I do not mean to say that you must lack any feeling. This happens only much later. But I am saying that the strength of God is so great in you that the pains which reach you need not make an impression on you. Remain outside and do not enter into the experience of the pain of insults.

I say that one must be completely humble, strong and patient to live unknown among the best of men and be known by God alone. Actually, the number of these really humble souls is so small that it is difficult to meet even one of them. That is why the best thing is to be perfectly alone as much as possible—as much for the body as for the spirit. One must be dead to anything created, in order to be known only by God—in one's ways, in one's spirit, in one's intentions, in one's works, words and actions. It is better to be thought indiscreet and careless than to try to justify oneself and excuse oneself. But comparing oneself with those who are full of wisdom in their own eyes and are curious and subtle examiners searching the spirit, we must not do that.

Furthermore, the man who is really humble never thinks about himself or his holiness. He thinks he is the lowest of the low and expects incessantly that he would be treated as such, according to the eternal order of God though whom he lives and with whom he dies, always happy with whatever happens to him. He never thinks about himself in order to find himself, nor about others. And if they treat him badly he accepts any bad treatment. And he does that through the love he bears for his Lord, always thinking he himself is very small.

Those who are humble at heart and in spirit are very happy, so those who mistreat them surely believe that these humble people with whom they amuse themselves do not suffer pain. Or they think the reason these people have broken hearts about the cruelties put upon them is because they cannot get their revenge straightaway, or that they behave in this way through sheer hypocrisy. Such people do not understand things of the spirit.

159

Those who live by the spirit are easily known by their evenness of temper, constancy and immobility, and also by the fact that they are never touched or moved by emotion inside, no matter what happens. They must be careful, however, that their holy freedom does not cover pride and real humility under the same veil. One way these lovely spirits can be distinguished is by the fact that they leave everything to God if someone thinks that their opinions are not right.

I have said somewhere that the freedom of those who are completely perfect is unreasonable, but it is not contrary to reason nor without reason. It is infinitely above any reason. It is more simple, enlightened and unique, and the spirit has risen above reasoning. This is made clear by the choice not to reflect. It is the duty of those who are really holy to leave everything and be what they really are in themselves.

From the author of
The Mystical Day

The fourth state of mind, which is very necessary to acquire wisdom, is humility. The Son of God said that he wanted the proud man to be more humble and the humble man to be elevated. Nothing is greater than God, and there can be nothing more sublime for a Christian than to be able to get nearer to God or to be united to Him.

Saint Augustine said that if you are trying to rise, to reach through your highest thoughts the knowledge of God, you will find that He goes ever further away from you. But if you become humble under His powerful hand, He comes nearer to you.

It is through humility, through annihilation, through absence of light, through quick obedience to God's will, and through love that God wants to introduce you to the secret of His face. Ask God for complete death to yourself through humbling and enslaving of your mind. Ask Him to make you like a child.

All these teachings cannot reveal to you the secret of your nothingness and your humility. Pray "Oh, if You Yourself, oh my God, come down from the highest heaven, You can teach me." This is the way to enter into true humility and learn to be continually dependent on God. Say to God through the words of a great prophet: It is You, oh my God, who does everything within me. I only annihilate little by little my movements in order to let Your life live through me.

23

INDIFFERENCE TO CIRCUMSTANCES

Here are my comments found in
A Short and Simple Way to Pray

Please see more on this subject under the topic of Abandonment.

Practically, the believer must be continuously losing all his will in the will of God. He must renounce all particular inclinations, however good they appear to be, as soon as he feels that they are surfacing. He must do this to put himself into a state of indifference, to want nothing but the will of God—to be indifferent to everything, whether for the body or for the soul, whether for eternal or temporal good.

He must also accept all states which it will please God to put him in, accepting everything that He gives: enlightenment or darkness, facility or sterility, strength or weakness, sweetness or bitterness, temptation or distraction, sufferings, worries, uncertainties. Nothing must stop the believer.

The Song of Songs

I must only wish for His will, and be indifferent to His coming and goings. I must admit that my love is selfish although I did not know this. I used to prefer the pleasure I had in loving Him to His own pleasure. I liked to see Him and to possess Him. The lover I want to be is so detached that I could neither incline towards possession nor towards deprivation. I would care less about life or death. Although my love is strong, still I would not even wish for heaven.

Francis of Sales

Saint Francis makes a wonderful comparison between an excellent musician who, although he had become deaf, kept on playing his lute wonderfully. Since he did not derive any more pleasure from it because he could not hear, he only sang to give pleasure to his prince who sometimes put him to test. After having ordered him to sing, the prince would leave him, but the musician went on. He had neither any pleasure of the tune from which he was deprived of hearing, nor pleasure of pleasing the prince, since the prince was not there enjoying the beautiful tunes he was playing.

The human heart is the true musician of the song of sacred love. It is the harp and the maker of psalms. This musician usually listens to himself and takes great pleasure in listening to the melody of his song. That is to say, his heart loving God enjoys the pleasure of this love. This needs to change—however paradoxical that may seem to be.

Instead of loving God only because He is the Beloved, we love because the love comes from us who are the lovers. Thus we do not seek God, but come to ourselves, loving love instead of loving our Beloved—loving this love not for the pleasure nor contentment of God, but for the pleasure and contentment which we get from it ourselves.

Oh God! Thus it is not to please you that this man wants to sing; it is because of the pleasure he gets from it.

A will resigned to the will of God must not have any will, but simply serve the will of God. Furthermore, the will of God is just as good, and sometime even better, in sickness than in health. If we prefer to be in good health, we must not say that it is in order to serve God better. It is easy to see that what we look for in the will of God is health—not the will of God in health.

I turn your attention to

John of the Cross

The believer we are talking about is calling for this dark secret place in God because, according to Saint Thomas, secret wisdom is poured into the believer by love. Understand, though, that this happens secretly and has nothing to do with the natural world of understanding or of other spiritual powers. Such spiritual powers cannot acquire this wisdom or love. The Holy Spirit must pour it into the soul without the person knowing how it happens, as the Bridegroom says in the Song of Songs.

In truth, the believer does not understand it because the Master who bestows it is inside the believer's spirit. As far as we can see, the believer has in his spirit these truths poured into his spirit by faith. In the same way as a drink spills over all the arms and legs and blood veins of the body, thus this fellowship from God usually spills onto the believer.

A Short and Simple Way to Pray

Giving up everything must concern the inner self as well as the outer self. Everything must be left in the hands of God. We must forget ourselves and think only of God. In this way the heart remains free, happy and disengaged.

As soon as the self weakens because of the spirit of God, a believer can feel in himself the proof that God is his Father. This testimony fills him with joy ever so much more now that he is called to the freedom that belongs to the children of God. Now he knows that the spirit he has received is not one of servitude, but of freedom. He feels that he acts freely and sweetly, although strongly, without feeling any guilt.

Someone will say to me that God never takes man's freedom away from him and thus man can always fight against God, and that, therefore, I must not say that God acts absolutely without man's consent.

To make things clearer, I am saying this: It is enough for man to passively consent so that he gives a passive agreement, so that he keeps complete freedom. He gave himself to God as soon as he started on this way, so that God could make of him and in him whatever He wished. So a believer, from the very beginning of putting his trust in the Savior, gives an active and general consent to whatever God would do in the future.

The Song of Songs

The believer means that, being in perfect freedom of the spirit and of the soul, since he does not have any private property and works only for the glory of God, thus he will give God all the fruit of his life.

Thomas A. Kempis

It is very rare to find a person who is completely free and whose purity is not tarnished by the stain of trying to find himself, that is, in his self.

I believe our Lord would say: Some abandon themselves to Me, but there is always some reservation. Since they do not trust Me completely they still try to take care of themselves. There are some who offer themselves completely to Me but, being led into temptation, they become master of themselves again. And thus they do not progress in spiritual growth.

These people never know what is the real freedom of a pure heart, nor do they know the sweetness and the grace that I give to the believer whom I invite into My divine intimacy. To experience these things they must first give up everything for Me without reservation, and make a continual sacrifice of all that they are. Without this no one can ever be perfectly reunited to Me nor enjoy Me.

Catherine of Genoa

These spirits who have become accustomed to divine love live in great freedom and do not care for all the things on the earth.

Oh Love! You make Your lovers annihilate themselves inside themselves, and then You make them free in Yourself. Their freedom is perfect and complete. They want to stay with You, Lord. They want only what God wants. Everything else is a serious impediment for them and a nuisance.

Theresa

His divine Majesty rewards us very liberally. We are not without payment or compensation. We may not know how we found such freedom of spirit, so precious, or where could be found all the happiness that we could ever desire in this life. Wishing for nothing, everything is ours. We fear nothing and wish for nothing of the things of this world. Work does not worry us and happiness does not rouse our emotions. Briefly, nothing can take our peace away from us because our peace depends on God alone, and nothing could take God from us.

John of the Cross

When a believer is at this stage of perfect life, he goes forth always joyful, as if it were a feast day. He enjoys God, and he sings a song always new, where joy and love mix. Since the Bride knows the high stage she has reached, sometimes she says with joy: "My glory will always be renewed; my days will be multiplied as those of the palm tree!"

Nicholas of Jesus-Maria

Nicholas extensively quotes many Roman Catholics who were sainted by the church. Here are quotes he has given us of Christians who came before us.

Rusbroche tells us what others have said. There is an inner freedom, that is, without images or figures or other hindrances, which a person can bring to God by his inner fellowship. The man whose prayer is centered only on his Lord becomes free and is rescued from everything. He is always naked in the secret of his inner self.

Saint Augustine tells us the man who fellowships intimately with Jesus Christ is like someone at the top of a high mountain where neither the clouds nor the winds can reach. The mountain climber can use his sight with more freedom and can imagine better the brightness and serenity of the sun because of the purity of the air and because of the calm and tranquil surroundings. In the same way, for as long as the believer is allowed to retain his high position without lowering himself to thinking of lower things, he will be able to realize with complete freedom divine reality. Men who pray in this way have their residence in the region of eternity and clarity, for they have been put outside any perturbances and outside the infinite confusion of desires. They go on rising till they reach a serene atmosphere of liberty, and their life is as different from men who do not know Christ as the latter are different from animals.

Saint Gregory: Jubilation is the inexpressible joy of the spirit which cannot be hidden and cannot be expressed in words.

John of Saint Samson

In order that the man who lives inwardly may continue to enjoy his heart and all his spiritual realities, elevated over everything that has to do with the senses, and in order that everything should be just and straightforward, this believer must be master of his emotions. Then he will enjoy true freedom.

We must now speak about the true and perpetual joy of lovers who continually enjoy themselves in their unity with each other, as is experienced between a believer and his Lord through the practice of faith. The subject of this believer's perpetual joy is the total and infinite being of God. It is He who produces and makes any joy run through the Bride, through the fecund and abundant flowing of His divine fellowship. His presence fills her with joy and completely drowns her with divine delight.

The real freedom of truly spiritual people is misunderstood by those who do not have such freedom because of their pride.

Those who are completely abstracted and lost to themselves are pure spirits as far as their affections and feelings, and they cannot be caught as birds can be. Everything is only one thing to them in the abyss of life, and they get lost and engulfed in this abyss more and more. The active freedom coming out of those who are purely free covers their humility as a veil.

Those who have not grown to this point must be careful of feeling wounded or offended when they see the practical acts and words of those who are more spiritual and lost to themselves. When you tell them they are free, you have told them everything.

The Song of Songs

This believer must lose any interest in his salvation, his perfection, his joy, his

166

comfort. He must think only of what is God's interest. He will not ask anything for himself but ask only that God be glorified.

Catherine of Genoa

Catherine hated herself so much that she did not fear to say in this life, "I do not wish for grace, nor mercy, but justice." She did not try to gain indulgences, because she preferred that the part of her that offended God should be punished rather than to see herself in the presence of God absolved and delivered in such an easy way. Catherine did not even want to be prayed for by others because she was willing to bear all sorts of torments and even to be condemned as a criminal. She used to say, "Oh my Love, everything can be borne; but to have offended You, this is unbearable."

One day she was commanded by her judges: "Wake up, dead, and come to judgment!" She cried in a loud voice "I am more than willing to do that!" She believed that with His love that she felt in her heart, she could pass through any judgment, however narrow and hard it could be. She could see nothing in herself that was opposing this judgment. In fact, she was glad, wishing to be able to see this Divine Judge who is infinitely powerful, and in front of whom everything trembles except true and pure love.

Francis of Sales

We must adore, love and praise forever the vengeful and powerful justice of our God, even as we love His mercy, because both are daughters of His goodness. We must therefore agree with the divine will and show joy and equal reverence to the right hand of His mercy and the left hand of His justice.

John of Saint Samson

The believer we have been describing is pleased by nothing except to enjoy God completely, infinitely and eternally.

The dying life of self, laborious and very difficult, the believer must usually go through at great cost and often for a very long period of time. This first stage is as the believer gives his own life back to God. He passes through a very painful and bitter spiritual agony of which the mortal stages cannot be fully expressed. That is why man, externally and inwardly, must go back to God, which is the only way human beings can become His Bride.

It is very true, my God, that Your intimate friends do not think of what is just nor what is justice, nor about what is holy nor of what is holiness. They do not fear Your justice at all: for as You are all greatness, all love, all goodness, all wisdom, all power and all mercy, You are also all justice. And since Your justice rewards love by giving Yourself to us, it is this same justice which condemns those who are damned and who have caused their own damnation.

I cannot help including here the feeling of a shepherd related by Surin.

SurinA shepherd listening one day to the prophesy of the Day of Judgment, said "I wish it were today! I wish it were today!" I asked him why he was so joyful since the

167

greatest saints have always feared this last day because of the general judgment which will take place then. He said to me that the holy people who fear that day were motivated only by a selfish love. Wishing the damnation of those who were lost, they were considering only the severity of the Judge and what would happen to those who were lost.

"But as for me," said the shepherd, "I do not look at the interest which self-pride would push me to take, either my own damnation or theirs. I look simply at the interests of the Judge and the great joy of the elect. If I had no love for this just and loving Judge, I would not look forward to this particular day. This second coming of the Son of God should be even more wished for than the first coming because it is more advantageous than the first. At the first coming, it seems that the Son of God had renounced His greatness, since He annihilated Himself, taking the form of a servant. On the contrary, in this second coming He will come in possession of His double glory, that of the soul and of the body, no more degraded like a sinner or in the fragility of this mortal life, but living and ruling in His own majesty, glory, power, authority and that of God His Father.

"In this second coming He will come for Himself, and will be there for men and for angels in order to judge them. He will judge them for His glory and honor. If, therefore, I have even a little love for Him, should I not wish for this day to come soon, because it will be to His glory? I will add this, as well: Since we are obliged to love Jesus Christ, as Creator and Redemptor, more than ourselves, and to prefer His interest to ours, we must love His coming because it is all for the glory of Jesus Christ the Redemptor.

"If you knew," said this shepherd, "What glorious things would happen on that day, you would desire it as much as I do. I think that the divine Wisdom hides the glory of it from even the wisest people in the world, but He reveals it to those who have simple hearts.

"Today I adore with all my heart the sentencing which will come out of the mouth of my Judge and Redemptor, whatever He thinks of me. I do not know whether I will be able, at that time, to agree with His judgment. So I want right now to adore that judgment and renounce my own interest. I desire His glory more than my own happiness. I hate all my sins and want to condemn what He wants to condemn, to destroy what He will destroy, and go whichever way He wants."

He ended by saying: "Is there anyone who would not love this great day and wish for it if he loves Jesus Christ, since all this is for His glory. This is why I wish the day could be right now. I love it and adore it and everything that will happen on that day, even if it is at my own disadvantage, since it is for the advantage of the Father, the Creator; of the Son, the Redemptor; and of the Holy Spirit, the Sanctifier."

The Song of Songs

You know many mediocre people of whom ordinary praise well enough expresses their qualities. And you know of some who are so much above anything that can be said of them that no one can praise them worthily, but can only say that they are above all praises. Such is the divine Bridegroom, who makes His Bride voiceless, even when the Bride tries to praise Him in order to attract people's hearts and minds to Him. Her passion makes her try to express some praise suitable for a Bridegroom. However, she is ashamed to attempt to express His inexplicable merit. She takes refuge in silence, un-

You are my sister because we belong to the same Father. You are my Bride since I have already married you. Our marriage will be very soon consummated.

As soon as the Bride has abandoned everything, she is well prepared to go into the wedding bed of the Bridegroom where, having hardly got into it, she is enjoying the sacred and chaste delights of the kiss on the mouth which she has always desired, and which she now possesses because of the essential union which she has just been granted. She cannot help but express her happiness: "I belong completely to my Beloved, and my Beloved is completely mine!" Or, in other words: Oh, inexplicable advantage! I will only say this, that I completely and entirely belong to my Beloved, and I possess Him without hindrance or restriction.

God is in her and she is in God and they are one, since by the consummation of the marriage she has flown into God and finds herself lost in Him. And she cannot find herself again.

The marriage of bodies, through which two people become one flesh, is only an approximate symbol for this union, through which, as Saint Paul says, God and the believer become only one spirit.

One always wonders when the spiritual wedding will take place. It is easy to see by what we have been saying. The engagement, or mutual promise, is done in the union of spirits. The believer gives himself to God, and God gives Himself completely to the believer, in order to unite Himself with the believer. This is an agreement and a reciprocal promise. But, alas, there is quite a way to go. There is a lot of suffering to endure before this so-wishful union could be accomplished and consummated!

The marriage is done when the believer finds himself dead between the arms of the Spouse, who receives him in His union. But the consummation of the marriage is only accomplished when the believer is so melted and annihilated that he can, without reservation, flow into God. Then an admirable mixing of creature with his Creator unites them, although there is as infinite a disproportion between them as there is between a drop of water and the sea. Although the drop of water has become the sea, it remains always a small droplet mixed into the whole of the sea, to become a sea with it.

I turn your attention to

Harphius

In order to get the Bridegroom's sacred kiss, she must love chastely, that is to say, she must love only her Bridegroom, must ask for nothing or look for nothing outside of Him. She must love ardently, that is to say, to be so intoxicated with the love of her Bridegroom that she thinks only of His Majesty.

Theresa

When it pleases our Lord to have mercy on what the believer has endured and is still enduring, He puts the believer in His house. Because of the believer's ardent desire, He has already taken him or her for His Bride. Then, even before the spiritual marriage is consummated, she is received into the Father's house.

169

What God communicates to the human spirit in an instant is such a great secret and such a sublime favor that I cannot think of anything to compare it to. The spirit of the believer becomes similar to the Spirit of God. God wished to show the love He has for us by letting some people see the limits of His mercy, so that we can bless and praise His greatness. So He lowers Himself to unite with this creature. He does not want to be separated from the believer; as there is no separation between people who are married.

It is as if the water from the sky is falling in a river or in a fountain, where all the water is mixed, so that one cannot distinguish the falling rain from the water of the earth. Or it is as if a small stream entered into the sea, from which it cannot be separated anymore. Or as if in a room there were two windows through which entered a great light, and although this light came into the room divided in two different directions, still they are only one light. This is perhaps what Saint Paul means by these words: "The ones who belong to the Lord become one spirit with Him."

John of the Cross

God, in order to make us understand the high stage of unity that Moses had reached, says of Moses, "I talk to him face-to-face, and he sees the Lord not as an image, but openly." By this he wants us to know that, at this high stage of union, God does not communicate with the believer under any kind of disguise or imaginary vision, but mouth-to-mouth to the pure and naked essence of the believer's spirit.

Then we must know that some people get to the early stages, each according to how perfect their love is. But few people in this life reach this last and more inner stage. That is the stage of perfect union with God, which is called spiritual marriage. What God communicates to the believer in this union is nearly inexpressible, so one cannot say what it is like. It is God Himself who communicates with the believer and transforms him with admirable glory, both of them becoming one. The oneness is like the window pane with the rays of the sun, or of coal with fire, or the light of the stars with the light of the sun. Even this unity, of course, is not perfect, as it will be in the next life.

And thus, to make us understand what such a believer receives in this union, he does not say, and I don't think he can say, anything more than these words: "I drank of my Friend without difficulty."

Spiritual marriage between a believer and the Son of God is much more than the engagement, because it is a complete transformation in the being who loves. Two people give themselves to each other, each possessing the other, through a perfect and consummated union of love in which the human spirit becomes one with God. It is the highest stage which can be reached while we are on this earth. As in the consummation of the human marriage, both parties become only one flesh according to what Holy Writ says. In the same way, in this spiritual marriage between God and the believer, having been consummated, two natures are joined in one spirit in the love of God. It is just as when the light of a star or of a candle joins the light of the sun to be united with its light. The sun is the one which gives the light, hiding or absorbing in itself the other sources of light.

The Bride in the Song of Songs enjoys her Friend in the inmost place, where He is united with her in love and where she enjoys Him secretly. And the things that happen

170

in this fellowship, in the marriage with her Beloved, are so high and so wonderful that she could not express them and would not want to either. For these things are those which Isaiah mentioned: "My own secret, my own secret." And thus the believer possesses God alone, hears Him alone and enjoys Him alone, and takes pleasure in the fact that these things are done between themselves alone.

"There you will show me all that my soul . . .(had previously tried to understand)."

There is a dilemma in the equality, or union, of love. The Lover cannot be content if He does not feel and see that love is given as it is received, and vice versa, reciprocally. The believer sees the immensity of the love of God, and he would like if he could to love Him as much as He loves and as perfectly. For this, the believer desires to be actually transformed, so that his will can merge with that of God. In order to do this, the two wills must unite in such a way that out of the two only one emerges. As the Apostle says: "I live, but it is not I who lives, but Jesus Christ lives in me." And thus, in this sense there is equality of love because the will of the believer has become the will of God. Therefore, the believer loves God with the love of God. This will of God in the sense mentioned above is also the will of the believer. It comes from the fact that this very sublime love is inspired by the Holy Spirit. The same Apostle says: "The love of God is given to us by the Holy Spirit who has been given to us."

This means that God gives the believer the love with which the believer will love Him. It is as if God puts the right tools into the believer's hands and tells him what to do. And thus at this stage the believer loves God with a very high sort of love similar to the kind of love with which God loves the believer. The believer is taught how to love and becomes very good at it, being united with the very Master who teaches him or her to love. Therefore, the believer remains content and satisfied, but he does not become so until he reaches this kind of love—which is to love God perfectly with the same love with which He Himself loves.

We cannot reach perfection in this life, although in the state of perfection which is spiritual marriage, which we are talking about, it can be experienced to some extent. And from this perfect love is born a wonderful and intimate joy in God which plunges the believer into glory and draws forth praise to God. The believer feels a kind of urge which makes him praise, revere, and magnify God with great joy and love. This only happens when God gives the believer in this stage of transformation a great purity, such as that of the state of innocence before the Fall, or the state we are in when we are redeemed.

James of Jesus

tells us:

Saint Bernard says to the monks of Mont-Dieu that there is still another likeness of God which is so natural to the believer that it is not called resemblance anymore, but unity of spirit. Man is made one spirit with God, not only by the union of wills, but by another union—the virtue of not being able to wish for anything different. Now this union is called unity of spirit not only because it is accomplished by the Holy Spirit, but because the Holy Spirit touches the spirit of man. Also because the Holy Spirit Himself,

God in His mercy, gives to man a unity of substance with God—the same unity which exists between God the Father and God the Son. In an extraordinary way, man who does not deserve it is made by grace what God is by nature.

To have been granted grace is like being engaged. It is to love truly. It is for the believer to resolve never to separate himself from the divine will. This union, which the mystics call spiritual marriage, is not only to communicate affection. It is a very narrow communication between people, although there are acts of love and goodness. In this union God communicates in the Trinity with an extraordinary love, and the Father and the Son send the Holy Spirit. So the believer, as Bride, participates in all the goodness of God, and the Persons of God belong to the believer who participates here with all the goodness of God by love. And the Holy Spirit (because He proceeds from the Father and the Son), having been sent from Them to the believer, becomes in this very divine union just what He is in substantial unity between the Father and the Son. Therefore, the Holy Spirit is present in the believer's spirit with love, sweetness, goodness.

This is substantially what Saint Bernard wants to say, and it is not without reason that he calls this union perfect unity of spirit. This same Holy Spirit, who is the love of the Father and the Son, is sent to the believer's spirit to be his goodness and to communicate the love of God to the believer's heart.

John of Saint Samson

Ah! Who is the bride who would not be ravished in the love of her bridegroom, after having been received by the deepest and most delicious embraces! The bride who has received the kiss on the mouth from her bridegroom! Who has been plunged into admirable delights, such as those which come from reciprocal love? Show me I am wrong if you can, well beloved brides, who have experienced such a thing. But let me know if there are delights, transfusions, transports, ecstasies, embraces, and loves like the love of God!

A Short and Simple Way to Pray

One could object that by this way one would not really know the mysteries. It is completely the opposite. They are indeed given to the believer. Jesus Christ is given and is chosen as the way, is heard as truth, and gives life. He makes His mark on the believer and, in so doing, designates him for His own. To be with Jesus Christ at all times is something much greater than to only think about Jesus Christ. Saint Paul had been destined to follow Christ: "I carry on my body the marks of Jesus Christ." That is very different from saying that he was *thinking* about Him.

Often Jesus Christ, when the believer has abandoned everything for Him, gives some specials signs. We must accept them and accept whatever pleases Him, while at the same time accepting whatever conditions He will please to put us in. We must not try to choose our own situation, except that of staying near to Him, to annihilate ourselves before Him. We must receive all that He gives us, light or darkness, facility or sterility, strength or weakness, sweetness or bitterness, temptation, or distraction, suffering, worrying, being uncertain—nothing of all this must stop us.

There are some people who God allows to taste one of His mysteries for many years. The very thought of this mystery makes them turn inward. We hope they will be faithful to it, but when God takes it away from them they must accept it.

Others worry that they cannot perceive any mystery. It does not matter, since God's attention implies a special devotion, and whoever is united to God because he takes his rest in Him has much better than any mystery. Who loves God loves whatever comes from Him.

Nicholas of Jesus-Maria

He tells us that Saint Bonaventure said: Jesus Christ hides Himself from our view when we try, with the eyes of the mind, to see the Wisdom from above. We must enter into the darkness and the night.

John of Saint Samson

When you are filled with the sweetness of love, you will feel what it means to be hindered by signs and visions and created things. Through the loving exercise of aspiring to Him, you will get rid of such hindrance, and will stay naked, simple, calm, and free inside yourself. You will be like a well-polished mirror reflecting naively the perfection and the beauty of God and the sacred human form of our dearest and beloved Savior and Bridegroom. Thus you will be, inside and outside, a faithful lover who is always in the presence of God her Beloved.

Louis, Abbot of Estival

Louis tells us about a woman who exposed to her spiritual guide her doubts about seeking to understand mysteries, and she herself proposed how to resolve her problem. She said, "All the preachers and all the good books teach that we must meditate on the mysteries of our Lord. However, the believer who has reached a high stage is incapable of doing so. It seems to me, however, that this person accomplishes the same purpose by actually representing the mysteries. Since God is infinite in greatness, contains all mysteries, and is in possession of this believer, the believer has the essence of the mysteries."

The Song of Songs

The Bridegroom gives His lover some very good instructions: If you do not know yourself, He says to her, disappear. He means to say that she could not possible know the divine Object of her love, however passionately she wishes it, if she does not know herself, since the annihilation of the self helps in knowing the Whole of God.

The Bride must reach a higher level and forget about everything, in order to come in with Me, in the bosom of My Father, and take rest there, having given up all her own ways.

But come also from the den of the lions and from the mountains where there are leopards: for it will only be through the most cruel persecutions, as from many savage beasts, that you will be able to reach such a divine stage. It is time to rise more than ever above all this since you are ready to be crowned as my spouse.
Her Beloved possesses her perfectly in her essence and in her spirit, beyond time and above all places.

I turn your attention to

Catherine of Genoa

I do not want of love which is for God nor in God. I cannot bear this word "for," nor this word "in," because it shows that there is something between God and me, something that is not pure love and cannot last. The love of God is the greatest and the purest because it is God Himself.

John of the Cross

The aim the believer tries to reach is above all things. It is the highest knowledge, the most sublime delight he can have in this life. "Above all things" means he must get to a non-knowledge state. He must forget having "a way" to reach his goal, which has no way, but is God Himself. The believer who has reached this stage has neither ways nor means, and he does not consider them and cannot consider them. I say that this believer has left behind all ways of understanding, of enjoying, and of feeling, although these means are still within him as someone who has nothing and possesses everything. Having the courage to go from his limited nature, he enters into limitless spirit, which has no ways but contains all ways. To reach this height is to leave nature and to go away from our lowly state.

The Wisdom of God, into which the human intelligence must be submerged, has no ways or means and does not fall under the limitations of intelligence. In order to be joined in perfect union, these two extremes—the believer and divine Wisdom—must have some kind of similarities between them. Hence, the believer must be pure and simple.

Not only does God lead the believer into the love of this solitude, but He Himself works in the believer without any particular way. It is one of the qualities of this union between the believer and God in the spiritual marriage, that God communicates directly with the believer, not through angels, as before. Inner and outer senses and all created things, even the believer himself, are not of any value when the believer is granted the mystical favors that God gives him. Neither his cleverness nor his faithfulness matter. God alone gives him that particular grace.

This union, although immense, is very subtle. Although communicative, it is also subtle and delicate. Therefore, oh delicate touch, you are very subtle and pure, and very simple, although being infinite and also infinitely delicate! Bright flame of love!

Benoit of Canfield

Although there is no human way of seeing the essence of spiritual unity, it has been proven that it exists. There is no active or actual way of reaching this unity (no action on the part of man, that is). However, there is a passive way: Man does nothing. I call it a way without a way. It is a way because it brings us to our goal. Still since the soul is passive, it is not a spiritual way, since any spiritual way means man doing something. This could be called a divine mean. Only God does something and the believer only suffers. Thus, he is immediately united to God without any ways. The rising of the spirit which happens through ignorance is moved through ardent love without any human help.

A Short and Simple Way to Pray

The destruction of our being proclaims the Sovereign Being of God. We must cease to be, so that the Spirit of the Word should be in us, or so that He should come to us. We must give our life to Him, and die to ourselves, so that He Himself lives in us.

We must leave our being to go into Jesus Christ, and we must cease living so that He can live in us and, being dead, our life must be hidden with Him in God.

Jesus Christ says that He "has life in Himself." All other beings are only borrowed life, but the Word has life in Himself. As He wants to communicate, He wants to communicate His life to man. Therefore, we must let this life flow into us, which can only happen if we lose the life of Adam, and cease our own action. As Saint Paul assures us: If someone lives in Jesus Christ, he is a new creature. Everything that belongs to the former creature has disappeared. Everything has become new. This can only happen in the death of ourselves and of our own action, so that the action of God can be substituted for ours.

It is impossible to reach spiritual union through any one way of worship or through some luminous prayer.

The Song of Songs

The priests who confess us should have died to themselves, having been crucified with Jesus Christ. They should teach the people they confess how to renounce themselves, to crucify themselves and to die to everything in order to live in God Himself and allow Christ to live in them.

The Bridegroom asks His spouse to get out of herself by renouncing herself. She is also to be faithful in everything.

The Bride finds herself in solitude so strange that, not finding her Bridegroom, she doesn't know what to do. Outside everything is dead to her. It is this separation from the creation and from all that is not God which makes the Bride beautiful in the eye of her Bridegroom.

The rains of winter have gone. The Bride can go out without fearing the winter, and she now has an advantage. The winter has destroyed and killed what used to be alive for her . . . and would have killed her also. It is like the way the severity of winter rids the earth of insects.

The marriage takes place when the Bride finds herself dead and expiring in the arms of the Bridegroom who sees her now better prepared, and receives her into His union.

The Bridegroom asks, at three different times, that His beloved should not be awakened. The first time she is sleeping a sleep of violent ecstasy which concerns the senses. The Groom prays that she should not be awakened because this sleep comes at the right time for her and helps to detach the senses from whatever part of creation they are attached to.

The second kind of sleep is the sleep of mystical death, where the Bride expires into the arms of love. God does not want her awakened until she wakes up by herself through the ever-powerful voice of God, who calls her from the tomb of death to a spiritual resurrection.

Catherine of Genoa

Love would come back to me again, saying: I want you to shut your inner eyes, so that you cannot see me doing things to you. I want you to be dead, and in you anything visible should be annihilated. I do not want you to try anything or do anything that you can feel yourself. I want you to look at yourself as if you had no being.

I could not keep totally quiet, staying like an immobile thing, because Love made me tight inside. I felt such a happiness and such an inner peace that I could hardly bear it. I did nothing but sigh and cry without speaking and without bothering to wonder how things were going. I felt dead inside. However, Love was saying to me: You feel that you can hardly bear yourself? What is wrong with you? I do not want you to sigh nor to cry, nor to complain. If you have any king of feeling, you are still alive. I want you to be like the dead, or like those who are ready to die. In fact, I do not want to see in you any sign of life.

Thus, being again enslaved by Love, I was not doing anything either inside or outside, which anyone could notice. When something resembling what I was feeling was talked about, I listened intently, hoping to hear something that would apply to me. But Love was saying that such sight, such hearing, did not please Him because these are all excuses, resisting and fleeing in front of death. I did not know what to do nor to say at such subtle ideas.

He gave me so many sufferings that the human part of me could hardly take food. I ate very little or nothing. One day I said to my confessor: "Shouldn't I try to eat, lest by not eating I should find myself in a state that would be bad for my soul or for my body?" Inside, Love answered me, as did the confessor outside. Nobody is obliged to force himself to eat or to force himself not to eat because of scruples.

When this particular part of me was caught in doing bad things, and when I could not deny any longer my imperfections which Love had discovered, I turned toward Him and said to Him: "Since Your views are so subtle and Your power so great, I give up. And although the physical part of me suffers from it, I accept everything according to Your will, which is to take away from me the bad dress of pride, oh great, ardent and fiery Lover!"

John of the Cross

Oh gentle hand! Even more gentle for me, for You are touching me gently. How formidable You could be for me if You wanted to weigh down on me. You make the earth tremble just by looking at it. Nations tremble and mountains fall down! Oh, gentle hand, how hard and rigorous for Job, because You touched him so roughly. But You

176

have touched my soul very graciously. You are so gentle and sweet to me, though You were hard and savage to him. You have touched me and given me Your love, but You struck him hard. You kill and You give life. There is no one who can escape Your hand. But You, oh Divine Life, only kill in order to give life. You only wound in order to cure. You have made me sad, oh divine hand, in order to cure me. You have killed in me what kept me dead without the life of God. In His life I now live. Bright flame of life!

There are two kinds of life. One of them is resurrected life, when we can see God. This life has to be preceded by a temporal death of the body. Saint Paul says, "We know that if our earthly house disappears we have a building in God, a house not made by the hand of man, an eternal house in heaven."

The other kind of life is the spiritual and perfect kind of life, which is a possession of God through a union in love. This kind of life can be acquired through death to the self. Until this is done, one cannot reach the perfect stage of union with God. According to what Paul says, "If you live according to the flesh, you will die; but if through the spirit you crucify the flesh, you will live." In this passage we must note that what is called death means all that the old man is. That is to say, you must annihilate memory, intelligence and will power. All these are used for terrestrial things and appetites. All these are things from your former life, which is dead. You live in a new life, a spiritual life, in which you could not live perfectly if you did not give up the old man.

As the philosophers say, the believer acting in God, because he is united to Him, lives from the life of God, and death becomes life.

The believer says: "By killing, you have changed death into life." The believer can now say with Saint Paul: "I am not myself, Jesus Christ lives in me." Thus what there is of death and of cold in this believer is changed into the life of God. The believer is absorbed into the life of God. So the words of the apostle are accomplished: "Death is absorbed into victory." Osee has written: "'Oh, death, I will be the death of you!' says the Lord."

Francis of Sales

In the French language we speak in a very particular way about death. We call it leaving this life. And we call the dead those who have left this life. Death in men is only a passage from one life to the next, and to die is only to go beyond the limits of this mortal life and go to the immortal one.

John of Saint Samson

There is a great difference between to die and to be dead. Dying in detail, little by little, one acquires the habit of humility, and humility becomes the person's close companion. The mystics tell us that three things are proper for a dead man. They are, to be buried, to have people tread on him until the day of judgment, and to be reduced to ashes.

A very low state belongs to a dead person. I say that the three aspects of death mentioned before are: being buried, then rotting, and from rottenness to become ashes. These are the stages nearest to nothing. But even nothing is not nothingness.

The mystics tell us the three things proper for someone who is dead: He must be entombed, he must be put in the ground and people must walk over him until the day of judgment, and he becomes ash. One could not express better that dead people cannot feel. This is a sign that dead people are completely dead as to their own nature. Men will do what they like with us. And when they do what they like with us we will not protest. Good men who are dead and those who are dying are in two very different states. It is true that those who are on the point of death are very near it, as it is true that some people are on the point of dying longer than others.

The Bride must be very careful not to look for death, the death of the senses. She must live here quite lost to herself, not knowing that she is living in this noble state, in order to please the One she wants to please forever, in her perpetual and deep death which unites her to Him, truly and totally.

ENDING

After submitting this manuscript to Bishop Bossuet she remained under house arrest at a convent near his church in Meaux. Later the other two priest who made up the court of inquiry ruled that Guyon was innocent of "novel" or heretical teachings.

Bossuet was enraged. He refused to allow Guyon to go free. A few months later he released her. As soon as she departed, he accused her of escaping. Guyon was arrested in Paris and imprisoned.

So, effectively ended the earthly ministry of Jeanne Guyon. So also began a sought after ministry-in-writing - unparalleled in church history.

SeedSowers

P.O. Box 3317
Jacksonville, FL 32206
800-228-2665

904-598-3456 (fax)   www.seedsowers.com

REVOLUTIONARY BOOKS ON CHURCH LIFE

The House Church Movement *(Begier, Richey, Vasiliades, Viola)* 9.95
How to Meet In Homes *(Edwards)* 10.95
An Open Letter to House Church Leaders *(Edwards)* 4.00
When the Church Was Led Only by Laymen *(Edwards)* 4.00
Beyond Radical *(Edwards)* 5.95
Rethinking Elders *(Edwards)* 9.95
Revolution, The Story of the Early Church *(Edwards)* 8.95
The Silas Diary *(Edwards)* 9.99
The Titus Diary *(Edwards)* 8.99
The Timothy Diary *(Edwards)* 9.99
The Priscilla Diary *(Edwards)* 9.99
The Gaius Diary *(Edwards)* 9.99
Overlooked Christianity *(Edwards)* 14.95

AN INTRODUCTION TO THE DEEPER CHRISTIAN LIFE

Living by the Highest Life *(Edwards)* 8.99
The Secret to the Christian Life *(Edwards)* 8.99
The Inward Journey *(Edwards)* 8.99

CLASSICS ON THE DEEPER CHRISTIAN LIFE

Experiencing the Depths of Jesus Christ *(Guyon)* 8.95
Practicing His Presence *(Lawrence/Laubach)* 8.95
The Spiritual Guide *(Molinos)* 8.95
Union With God *(Guyon)* 8.95
The Seeking Heart *(Fenelon)* 9.95
Intimacy with Christ *(Guyon)* 10.95
Spiritual Torrents *(Guyon)* 10.95
The Ultimate Intention *(Fromke)* 11.00

IN A CLASS BY THEMSELVES

The Divine Romance *(Edwards)* 8.95
The Story of My Life as told by Jesus Christ *(Four gospels blended)* 14.95
Acts in First Person *(Book of Acts)* 9.95

COMMENTARIES BY JEANNE GUYON

Genesis Commentary 10.95
Exodus Commentary 10.95
Leviticus - Numbers - Deuteronomy Commentaries 12.95
Judges Commentary 7.95
Job Commentary 10.95
Song of Songs *(Song of Solomon Commentary)* 9.95
Jeremiah Commentary 7.95
James - I John - Revelation Commentaries 12.95

THE CHRONICLES OF THE DOOR *(Edwards)*

The Beginning 8.99
The Escape 8.99
The Birth 8.99
The Triumph 8.99
The Return 8.99

THE WORKS OF T. AUSTIN-SPARKS

The Centrality of Jesus Christ 19.95
The House of God 29.95
Ministry 29.95
Service 19.95
Spiritual Foundations 29.95
The Things of the Spirit 10.95
Prayer 14.95
The On-High Calling 10.95
Rivers of Living Water 8.95
The Power of His Resurrection 8.95

COMFORT AND HEALING

A Tale of Three Kings *(Edwards)* 8.99
The Prisoner in the Third Cell *(Edwards)* 5.99
Letters to a Devastated Christian *(Edwards)* 5.95
Healing for those who have been Crucified by Christians *(Edwards)* 8.95
Dear Lillian *(Edwards)* 5.95

OTHER BOOKS ON CHURCH LIFE

Climb the Highest Mountain *(Edwards)* 9.95
The Torch of the Testimony *(Kennedy)* 14.95
The Passing of the Torch *(Chen)* 9.95
Going to Church in the First Century *(Banks)* 5.95
When the Church was Young *(Loosley)* 8.95
Church Unity *(Litzman, Nee, Edwards)* 14.95
Let's Return to Christian Unity *(Kurosaki)* 14.95

CHRISTIAN LIVING

The Autobiography of Jeanne Guyon 14.95
Final Steps in Christian Maturity *(Guyon)* 12.95
Turkeys and Eagles *(Lord)* 8.95
The Life of Jeanne Guyon *(T.C. Upham)* 17.95
Life's Ultimate Privilege *(Fromke)* 10.00
Unto Full Stature *(Fromke)* 10.00
All and Only *(Kilpatrick)* 7.95
Adoration *(Kilpatrick)* 8.95
Release of the Spirit *(Nee)* 6.00
Bone of His Bone *(Huegel)* *modernized* 8.95
Christ as All in All *(Haller)* 9.95

* call for a free catalog 800-228-2665